DISCRIMINATION AGAINST NATIVE AMERICANS IN BORDER TOWNS

A Briefing Before the United States Commission on
Civil Rights Held in Washington, D.C.

Briefing Report

Table of Contents

EXECUTIVE SUMMARY

The U.S. Commission on Civil Rights has previously studied discrimination against Native Americans in communities next to American Indian reservations, frequently referred to as "border towns."[1] The Commission's state advisory committees (SACs), composed of voluntary members who advise the Commission on civil rights issues within their respective states, have been at the forefront of this effort.

In April 2004, the Commission's New Mexico State Advisory Committee held a forum in Farmington, a town bordering a Navajo reservation, to determine the prevalence of discrimination in the social and economic relationships of Native Americans and the white community. Thirty years earlier, the New Mexico SAC held a three-day open meeting and field investigation in Farmington after the homicides of three Navajo men at the hands of white teenagers near the city. The incident touched off a period of visible and dramatic protests by Indian organizations in Farmington designed to call attention to the condition of Navajos in the region. Its 1975 report examined issues relating to community attitudes; the administration of justice; provision of health and medical services; alcoholism; employment; economic development on the Navajo Reservation and its impact on neighboring border towns.

The New Mexico SAC's 2004 forum was designed to assess how conditions had changed in the area since the committee's 1975 report and included presentations from tribal leaders, state and local elected officials, community leaders, educators, representatives of law enforcement and business, and the general public. Based on this forum, the SAC submitted a November 2005 report to the Commission which concluded that though the intervening 30 years have witnessed an improvement with respect to the equal protection and enforcement of laws for Native Americans, tensions remain within the community, particularly with respect to Native Americans' interaction with law enforcement.

The Commission also received SAC reports from other states examining educational opportunity and the administration of justice for Native Americans in communities bordering their reservations.[2] For example, the Montana SAC analyzed disparities in education and offered recommendations for stemming high dropout rates for Native Americans (double those of non-Indian students), low achievement levels and test scores, and little advancement to higher education. A South Dakota SAC report chronicled anecdotal evidence suggesting that the administration of justice might be uneven for Native Americans, focusing on disparities in law enforcement stops, arrests, prosecutions, legal representation, and sentencing. According to the report, whether an unequal administration of justice existed or not, the perception of unfairness among Native Americans was so pervasive that it negatively

---

[1] Over the past few years, the Commission has also studied disparities in health outcomes of Native Americans, as well as their access to the same federally funded programs and services available to other Americans in areas such as housing, education, nutrition, and law enforcement. *See, e.g.* BROKEN PROMISES: EVALUATING THE NATIVE AM A QUIET CRISIS: FEDERAL FUNDING AND UNMET NEEDS IN INDIAN COUNTRY ERICAN HEALTH CARE SYSTEM (2004); A QUIET CRISIS: FEDERAL FUNDING AND UNMET NEEDS IN INDIAN COUNTRY (2003).

[2] *See, e.g.,* MONTANA ADVISORY COMMITTEE TO THE U.S. COMMISSION ON CIVIL RIGHTS, EQUAL EDUCATIONAL OPPORTUNITY FOR NATIVE AMERICAN STUDENTS IN MONTANA PUBLIC SCHOOLS (July 2001); SOUTH DAKOTA ADVISORY COMMITTEE TO THE U.S. COMMISSION ON CIVIL RIGHTS, NATIVE AMERICANS IN SOUTH DAKOTA: AN EROSION OF CONFIDENCE IN THE JUSTICE SYSTEM (Mar. 2000); SOUTH DAKOTA ADVISORY COMMITTEE TO THE U.S. COMMISSION ON CIVIL RIGHTS, NATIVE AMERICANS AND THE ADMINISTRATION OF JUSTICE IN SOUTH DAKOTA, Transcript of a Community Forum held Dec. 6, 1999 in Rapid City, South Dakota (Oct. 2000).

affected State-Indian relations, giving rise to an adversarial relationship between Indians and state and local law enforcement agencies and government. Furthermore, the South Dakota SAC report found that the state lacked adequate civil rights agencies and oversight mechanisms through which Native Americans could bring attention to their concerns.[3]

As part of its continuing assessment of progress in the conditions of Native Americans in border towns, the Commission held a November 9, 2007 briefing that included two panels of experts representing Native American reservations and the contiguous towns. The briefing was designed to examine recent changes for Native American communities on or off reservations. Specifically, the Commission was looking for policies, procedures, or events that have improved relationships between Native Americans and residents of border towns in local areas, and that could be implemented elsewhere. As part of this examination, panelists were asked to assess (1) the number of reported incidents of alleged discrimination against Native Americans in the communities selected for study; (2) the state of race relations in the selected communities, including both conflicts and efforts to alleviate tensions; (3) the ways in which perceived discrimination as inflicted, felt, and understood in border towns has changed over time; and finally, (4) how Native Americans' experiences in border towns differ from their experiences elsewhere in the country.

***

---

[3]*See* SOUTH DAKOTA ADVISORY COMMITTEE TO THE U.S. COMMISSION ON CIVIL RIGHTS, NATIVE AMERICANS IN SOUTH DAKOTA: AN EROSION OF CONFIDENCE IN THE JUSTICE SYSTEM 37 (Mar. 2000).

Summary of the Proceedings

Stephen Pevar

Stephen Pevar is an author of a book on the rights of Indians and tribes[1] and an attorney with the American Civil Liberties Union (ACLU) in Hartford, Connecticut. In his testimony, he asserted that racism against Indians is still pervasive today and is manifested daily in areas such as voting rights, education, law enforcement, and housing.[2]

Mr. Pevar described the American Civil Liberties Union (ACLU) Voting Rights Project which aims to enhance political participation of racial and language minorities and former prisoners.[3] Mr. Pevar stated that the organization has filed voting discrimination cases proving racial discrimination in Colorado, Nebraska, South Dakota, and Montana. He asserted that federal court decisions recognize that communities where school districts encompass portions of the reservation have deliberately and intentionally discriminated against Indian citizens.[4] He explained that border communities may elect school board members on an at-large basis, creating discrimination by preventing any Indian from ever being elected to the school board.[5]

Mr. Pevar discussed a 2006 ACLU lawsuit in Tripp County, South Dakota, *Antoine v. Winner School District*.[6] This case alleged race discrimination against Indians in the public school system that borders the Rosebud Sioux Indian Reservation and has a sizeable Indian population. As evidence for his claim of discrimination against Native Americans in schools, Pevar pointed to the racial disparity in disciplinary actions between 2001 and 2006 in the system's middle schools. He cited a statistic claiming that administrators suspended one in five Indian middle school students, but only one in 27 white pupils. He further noted that although Indians constitute only 20 percent of the population of the middle school, 60 percent of suspended students are Indian. He also cited racial imbalances in graduation rates as evidence of discrimination, noting that in 2003, only 11 percent of Indian children who entered the school as freshmen ultimately graduated. By comparison, he noted an 82 percent graduation rate for white students. He also claimed that Indian students were caught in what he termed "the school-to-prison pipeline" with school authorities allegedly treating Indian students' infractions of rules as violent acts constituting major threats to the school, while dismissing similar behaviors among white students. Between 2001 and 2006, he asserted that school officials referred 11 percent of Indian students to the police while referring fewer than one in every 50 white students.[7]

---

[1] See STEVEN PEVAR, THE RIGHTS OF INDIANS AND TRIBES (2002) or a later publication by the same title (2004). Also see the young-adult version of the same book entitled THE RIGHTS OF AMERICAN INDIANS AND THEIR TRIBES (1997).

[2] Cite details of his Murdo, SD clients here. *See* Briefing Transcript at 9-10.

[3] American Civil Liberties Union, "Voting Rights," p. 1, <http://www.aclu.org/votingrights/index.html> (last visited Feb. 21, 2008).

[4] *See, e g., Bone Shirt v. Hazeltine*, 336 F. Supp. 2d 976 (D.S.D. 2004); *Cuthair v. Montezuma-Cortez Colorado School District, No. RE-1*, 7 F. Supp. 2d 1152 (D. Colo. 1998); *Windy Boy v. Big Horn County*, 647 F. Supp. 1002 (D. Mont. 1986).

[5] *See* Briefing Transcript at 10.

[6] *See Antoine v. Winner School District* 59-2, No. 06-03007 (D.S.D. Mar. 27, 2006).

[7] *See id.* at 11–12.

Mr. Pevar reported that officials of the Winner, South Dakota, high school recently agreed to implement a remedial plan to settle the ACLU lawsuit and anticipated that the parties would urge the federal district court to adopt the plan (it did on December 10, 2007).[8]

Mr. Pevar also stated that a 2003 study of discrimination in rental housing in Montana, Minnesota, and New Mexico by the U.S. Department of Housing and Urban Development,[9] showed that American Indian families or individuals encounter discrimination 28.5 percent of the time. Mr. Pevar noted that the HUD study found that Indians were more likely than Hispanics, African Americans, and Asian Americans to experience racial discrimination.[10]

Frank Bibeau

Mr. Bibeau commented that Mr. Pevar's remarks accurately depicted the nature of discrimination in most reservations and raised similar concerns, including a discussion of alleged discrimination in the education, law enforcement and administration of justice contexts.[11]

With respect to discrimination in education, Mr. Bibeau alleged that the school board in Kelliher, Minnesota, which borders the Red Lake Indian Reservation, has adopted policies limiting class sizes in its schools to prevent Native American children from Red Lake from attending.[12] However, he focused on what he perceived as state encroachments into areas more properly regulated by tribal jurisdiction. For example, he complained that though reservation authorities issued identification cards that tribal members could use for voter identification in the elections, the state prevented tribal members from using that identification for other purposes, because the card did not have magnetic strips encoding personal information. He noted that in one area, county law enforcement officials dictated to local businesses what they could and could not consider as identification, despite local business owners' practices.[13]

According to Mr. Bibeau, the question of jurisdiction primarily affects law enforcement. He explained that a 1953 federal statute, Public Law 280,[14] mandated the shift of federal criminal jurisdiction over

---

[8] *See Antoine v. Winner School District* 59-2, No. 3:06-cv-03007-CBK (D.S.D. Dec. 10, 2007). On December 12, 2007, the judge in this case entered a consent decree to enforce this agreement.

[9] *See* MARGERY AUSTIN TURNER AND STEPHEN L. ROSS, WITH JULIE ADAMS, BEATA BEDNARZ, CARLA HERBIG, SEON JOO LEE, AND KIMBERLEE ROSS, THE URBAN INSTITUTE, DISCRIMINATION IN METROPOLITAN HOUSING MARKETS, PHASE 3 [NATIVE AMERICANS], prepared for the OFFICE OF POLICY DEVELOPMENT AND RESEARCH, U.S. DEPARTMENT OF HOUSING AND URBAN DEVELOPMENT (Sept. 2003), *available at* http://www.huduuser.ogr/publications/hsgfin/hds_phase3.html (last visited Feb. 21, 2008). *See also* News Release, HUD Study Shows More Than One in Four Native American Renters Face Discrimination, U.S. Department of Housing and Urban Development (HUD No. 03-126) (Nov. 17, 2003), *available at* http://www.hud.gov/news/release.cfm?content= pr03-126.cfm (last visited 21, 2008). David Melmer, *American Indians Face Rental Discrimination*, INDIAN COUNTRY TODAY (Dec. 19, 2003), *available at* http://www.indiancountry.com/content.crm?id=1071851594 (last visited Feb. 21, 2008); Mark Fogarty, *Study Uncovers Rental Discrimination*, INDIAN COUNTRY TODAY (Dec. 2, 2003), *available at* http://www.indiancountry.com/content.crm?id=1070388320 (last visited Feb. 21, 2008).

[10] *See* Briefing Transcript at 13–14.

[11] *See id.* at 15.

[12] *See* Briefing Transcript at 15-16.

[13] *See id.* at 15.

[14] Mr. Bibeau was most likely referring to Pub. L. No. 83-280, 67 Stat. 588 (1953); Briefing Transcript at 16–17.

offenses involving Native Americans in Indian country, as well as some civil matters, to the state in which the reservation resides. As a result, state law enforcement agencies and local sheriffs prosecute tribal members for criminal matters that occur within reservation boundaries in state courts (an exception is the Red Lake Reservation referenced earlier, a property which the Red Lake Band wholly owns). At the same time, most tribal governments also have their own criminal codes and courts.

According to Mr. Bibeau, the Supreme Court's 1987 decision in *California v. Cabazon*[15] upheld tribal authority over at least some civil matters, creating uncertainty or unpredictability for both tribal members and law enforcement.[16] To illustrate his point, Mr. Bibeau relayed an incident in which a Minnesota police officer stopped a young Native American whose vehicle had no license plates and who had no car registration, drivers' license or insurance—civil infractions which within the jurisdiction of tribal courts, not state. During the course of the stop, however, the officer found that the driver had been drinking and ticketed him for a DUI—a criminal offense in Minnesota.[17] Mr. Bibeau complained that because of the costs involved with referring individuals to tribal courts for civil violations, state officers often only write tickets and levy fines for infractions that are processed within the jurisdiction of state or municipal courts, thereby depriving tribal jurisdictions of the fines.[18] He further criticized what he perceived as the state's abuse of Public Law 280 in its use of civil forfeiture proceedings against cars belonging to those who had DUI offenses.

Mr. Bibeau suggested that tribal and county police also discriminate against Native Americans by agreeing that only tribal authorities will respond to emergency calls, not county police. He implied that this frees county officers in border towns from serving Native Americans on the reservation.[19]

In Bibeau's view, Public Law 280 has engendered considerable confusion, leaving people unsure of what laws the police will and will not enforce. To alleviate such difficulties, Mr. Bibeau recommended that Native Americans and their tribal governments take efforts to regain jurisdiction over criminal matters on Indian reservations.[20]

Mr. Bibeau identified both beneficial and unfortunate effects of the gaming industry on the economic well being of Native Americans. Frequently, the reservations' casinos are the largest county employers and the industry has raised the minimum wage to about $7.50 an hour, he said. The availability of such jobs enables many Native Americans to obtain credit and buy cars and houses, according to Bibeau. At the same time, because jobs in the gaming industry on reservations are often obtained as a matter of tribal political patronage, individuals are sometimes fired based merely on their family ties, losing income and creditworthiness. When that happens, he alleged that creditors in border towns view Native Americans' financial circumstances unfavorably as borrowers.[21]

The fragile economic circumstances of many Native American families contribute to difficulties in keeping them together, according to Mr. Bibeau. Because of the distances between reservations and

---

[15] *California v. Cabazon Band of Mission Indians*, 480 U.S. 202 (1987) (holding that under the facts of that case, the state did not have a compelling interest in prohibiting gaming on the reservation).

[16] *See* Briefing Transcript at 16.

[17] *See* Briefing Transcript at 17–18.

[18] *See id.* at 17-19, 22–23.

[19] *See id.* at 20–21.

[20] *See id.* at 16–17, 21.

[21] *See id.* at 20.

border towns, Native Americans must have a car to hold a job, keep a house, and hold families together. Mr. Bibeau explained that through a state-run program, called Children in Need of Protection or "CHIPs,"[22] courts have terminated parental rights and placed Native American children in adoptive homes where their parents were homeless or could not accommodate their children's special medical needs. He implied that job opportunities and modes of transport could have prevented such circumstances.

***

Panel One Discussion

The two panelists' discussion with the Commissioners focused on voting rights, law enforcement and the administration of justice, public schools, and social services.

Both Mr. Pevar and Mr. Bibeau elaborated on recent cases involving voting rights discrimination in response to questions from Commissioner Melendez. Mr. Pevar explained that the ACLU Voting Rights Project has handled cases in Thurston, Nebraska; Martin, South Dakota; northern South Dakota; Montana; and Colorado. All involved the county commissioner's office or a school district with a substantial Indian minority population concentrated in an area or a region within the voting district. Rather than selecting winners within each subdistrict, procedures called for choosing multiple candidates in a district-wide, at-large election. As a result, when the Indian population was less than 50 percent, as it was in the broader voting districts, Indians routinely lost the elections. They stated that all five cases resulted in federal court decrees finding that this arrangement constituted intentional discrimination.[23]

In an answer to Commissioner Melendez's request for more information about tribal enrollment cards, Mr. Pevar stated that obtaining voter identification is a national issue, not only for Indians but for other individuals who lack drivers' licenses. Native Americans have difficulty registering to vote if they do not have government-issued identification with a photograph. Mr. Pevar was aware of a number of Indians who had difficulty registering to vote, even with tribal identification cards.[24]

Mr. Bibeau agreed with Mr. Pevar's comments. Mr. Bibeau elaborated that a number of reservations worked in concert with the state to try to get tribal identification cards out to their members only to have state officials tell them a year later that the credentials lacked the magnetic strip with encoded information that The Homeland Security Act required. Mr. Bibeau explained that it was difficult to convince Native Americans to obtain and carry a card that would reveal their identity and residence. Yet state officials were now demanding that the identification card also have a magnetic strip with hidden

---

[22] *See* MINN. STAT. §260C.101 (2007).
[23] *See id.* at 26–27.
[24] *See id.* at 27–28. Currently, the State of Minnesota requires voters to have identification that verifies their residence, such as a valid Minnesota driver's license containing a valid address in the precinct or a tribal ID card that contains their name, signature, and address in the precinct.

information that many Indian people perceive with suspicion. In their eyes, the encryption is an invasion of privacy, likely providing the government an easier means of finding or mistreating them.[25]

Commissioner Yaki asked why officials in neighboring towns refuse to recognize the sovereign tribal nation's identification cards. Mr. Bibeau explained that the border towns' governmental institutions require citizens, including tribal members, to have credentials that their jurisdictions recognize, such as Minnesota drivers' licenses. He implied that these municipalities benefit from the fees they collect for issuing identification cards, such as the $18.50 cost of a Minnesota driver's license. Mr. Bibeau perceives such fee collection as a way of keeping Native Americans in poverty, especially because, in contrast, tribal identification cards cost very little now, and were formerly free. Because of the widespread poverty in Indian country, the burden of paying for the necessary identification is high, he said.[26]

Mr. Bibeau further implied that state officials' standards for Native Americans' identification for voter registration were discriminatory. He stated that when he has voted in predominately white districts, one needed only to present an electric bill showing an address for identification.[27] Mr. Bibeau hinted that requirements for identification are more stringent, but did not clarify whether he meant recently or for Native Americans.[28] [29]

Mr. Bibeau reported rumors on reservations that the [then] U.S. Attorney for the District of Minnesota[30] was examining voting rights issues, such as election turnout. The allegations apparently were that tribal members provide rides to the polls to people who do not possess cars or drivers' licenses, or help pay for gas for those who do own vehicles, and also whether similar trends occurred in off-reservation elections Mr. Bibeau said. However, he claimed the Native American population is not large enough to affect outcomes.[31]

Commissioner Yaki asked Mr. Pevar to describe the case that he had mentioned during his prepared remarks in which he believed the court's decision against a Native American was unfair. Mr. Pevar explained that he recently represented an Indian from the small town of Murdo, South Dakota, who was accused of possessing stolen property. Late one night, the man claimed, four Indian strangers stopped at his house and asked for $20, leaving a saddle with him as security. They promised to return later in the week and pick up the saddle. Such transactions are common in Indian culture, so the man agreed and gave the men the money. The strangers never came back. Three months later the client offered to sell the

---

[25] *See* Briefing Transcript at 28–29. In addition to the full legal name, signature, date of birth, gender, and an identification number, a card must have a facial photograph, the address of the principal residence, and encryption of information through a machine-readable technology.

[26] *See id.* at 30–31.

[27] *See id.* at 29.

[28] *See id. at* 29 and 31. Since the briefing, the Supreme Court in *Crawford v. Marion County Election Bd.,* 128 S. Ct. 1610 (2008) upheld a state law requiring voters to present photo identification before casting ballots. The Indiana Court of Appeals recently ruled that some provisions of the Indiana law that exempted absentee voters and residents of some licensed care facilities from having to produce state-approved identification violated the Equal Privileges and Immunities Clause of the state constitution. *See League of Women Voters of Indiana, Inc. v. Rokita*, 2009 WL 2973120 (Ind. Ct. App. Sep. 17, 2009).

[29] *See, e.g., Crawford,* 28 S. Ct. at 1643; Robert Barnes, *High Court Upholds Indiana Law On Voter ID; 6-3 Ruling Calls Measure Reasonable to Fight Fraud*, THE WASHINGTON POST, Apr. 29, 2008, at A1, A4; Stephen Dinan, *Court Upholds Requisite ID at Voter Polls; Risk of Fraud Trumps Burden*, THE WASHINGTON TIMES, Apr. 29, 2008, at A1, A10.

[30] At the time of this briefing the U.S. Attorney in Minnesota was Ms. Rachel Paulose. By email, Mr. Bibeau corrected his oral testimony during the briefing misidentifying this government official. Email communication dated April 2, 2010.

[31] *See* Briefing Transcript at 29–30.

saddle to a rancher who had horses. Recognizing the saddle as his own stolen property, the rancher called police, who arrested Mr. Pevar's client.[32]

At trial, Mr. Pevar called three prominent Indian witnesses who testified that in their culture people help one another without questioning them. The witnesses stated that they had given money to many needy Indian people, accepting personal property as collateral, and about half the time, the people came back for the property and the other half they did not. To prove this crime, Mr. Pevar suggested, the court would have to show intent, that is, that the defendant knew that the property was stolen when he took possession of it. Obviously he could not have known that the saddle belonged to the very person to whom he tried to sell it. According to Mr. Pevar, the evidence showed that the man's actions were reasonable within the Indian community. Another witness, a white woman who employed the defendant, testified that he was trustworthy and would not deliberately steal or possess stolen property. Yet, the jury announced a guilty verdict in less than an hour and a client Mr. Pevar believed was innocent was sent to prison for a year.[33] The next evening, when the white woman who had testified drove her car, the brakes failed. Her repair shop's mechanic determined that someone had slashed the brake fluid cable. Mr. Pevar stated that he and his legal aid colleagues routinely encounter such injustices.[34]

Mr. Bibeau related a personal experience as evidence of federal authorities' unfairness to the Indian people. Mr. Bibeau explained that when acting as a tribal attorney for the Leech Lake Reservation, a position he last held in 2004,[35] he served a lawsuit on the chief of police. Mr. Bibeau alleged that, in response, the police reported him to the FBI in Bemidji as an al Qaeda terrorist and attached a copy of the suit to the report. Mr. Bibeau implied that he was fired from his job because of this matter but did not learn about the report alleging that he was a terrorist until months later. When Mr. Bibeau approached the FBI agent in Bemidji about the matter, the agent reportedly acknowledged that he was not a terrorist, yet failed to disclose this information. Mr. Bibeau suggested that officials from the reservation's bordering towns deliberately undermine the Indian system to keep Native Americans in poverty.[36]

Commissioner Braceras and Vice Chairperson Thernstrom asked Mr. Bibeau for evidence to support his broad accusation that state or federal government officials prefer to keep Native American peoples impoverished and politically powerless. Mr. Bibeau replied that the result supports such a statement. He said the government has taken 98 percent of the United States' resources from Native Americans. It continues to try to gain the last two percent, in his view.[37]

Commissioner Melendez posed a query about how legal jurisdiction on or off the reservation affects the enforcement of criminal and antidiscrimination laws.[38] Mr. Pevar explained that whether the tribe, the state, or the federal government has jurisdiction over a particular crime depends on where the crime occurred (i.e., whether on or off Indian land), and the race of the victim as well as the race of the

---

[32] *See id.* at. 24.
[33] *See id.* at 24–26.
[34] *See id.* at 26.
[35] See Mr. Bibeau's biography in Appendix A.
[36] *See* Briefing Transcript at 40–41.
[37] *See id.* at 41–42.
[38] *See id.* at 31–32.

perpetrator.[39] The principles of criminal jurisdiction evolved from a host of court decisions and several federal statutes. Yet, unfortunately, many law enforcement agencies simply avoid spending time and other resources to prosecute violators on an Indian reservation. As a result, there is a vacuum in law enforcement.[40]

Mr. Pevar brought to the Commission's attention a recent Amnesty International report on violence against Native American women. It found that Native women on the reservation were two and a half times more likely to be raped than non-Native women off the reservation, and that the perpetrators were white men in the majority of incidents. Furthermore, there were no prosecutions in most cases.[41]

Mr. Pevar explained further that the federal government has jurisdiction on Indian reservations in criminal cases involving seven major crimes. (The list of crimes subject to federal prosecution has expanded over time.) As a result, any Indian or non-Indian, who commits a major crime against an Indian on the reservation, is prosecuted in federal court. He alleged that law enforcement officials fail to bring such cases. The nearest federal court and branches of the Federal Marshals Service and the Federal Bureau of Investigation (FBI) are 100 miles away from the Rosebud Reservation, for example. He alleged that federal authorities are simply reluctant to expend time and energy investigating even heinous crimes 100 miles from their home base.[42]

Commissioner Braceras questioned Mr. Pevar's explanation for the lack of prosecution of the crimes Native Americans commit. Rather than suggesting that police and courts do not want to spend time and money taking legal action in such cases or that they engage in discrimination, she suggested that federal authorities might have other reasons for the low number of prosecutions.[43]

Mr. Pevar first defended his statement of law enforcement's unwillingness to expend resources, and then admitted that there might be other reasons for the low rate of prosecutions, such as Indians' unwillingness to testify against others. Both Mr. Pevar and Commissioner Braceras agreed that one could not blame law enforcement for the lack of prosecution if witnesses will not come forward to testify. Commissioner Braceras suggested, and Mr. Pevar agreed, for example, that the unwillingness of witnesses to testify is common in domestic violence cases regardless of race. Nonetheless, Mr. Pevar still believed that the primary reason for the low number of prosecutions is that the U.S. Attorney's Office simply lacks the funds to bring many crimes to trial. The Amnesty International report offered this explanation as well, Mr. Pevar said.[44]

---

[39] *See id.* at 32. See "Chapter 8: Criminal Jurisdiction in Indian Country," in STEVEN PEVAR, THE RIGHTS OF INDIANS AND TRIBES 142-166 (2004).

[40] *See* Briefing Transcript at 32.

[41] *See id.* at 32–33.

[42] *See id.* at 33–34. Two applicable laws are 18 U.S.C. §1152, which grants jurisdiction to the federal government over crimes in Indian country except where: (1) an Indian commits an offense against the person or property of another Indian or on Indian land, or (2) an Indian has been punished by the local law of the tribe, or (3) to any case where, by treaty stipulations, exclusive jurisdiction is or may be secured to the Indian tribes respectively; and 18 U.S.C. §1153, which creates an exception to Section 1152, extending the federal government's jurisdiction to specified offenses such as murder, manslaughter, kidnapping, maiming, incest, felony child abuse or neglect, arson, and other serious crimes against any person committed by Indians within Indian country. Section 1153 further provides for state jurisdiction over any such offense not defined and punished by federal law.

[43] *See id.* at 34–35.

[44] *See id.* at 34–36.

Commissioner Braceras then suggested that the lack of resources hampers prosecutions not only of crimes on Indian reservations, but offenses across the state, including those in major cities and rural areas. Mr. Pevar agreed. He urged the Commission to look into prosecutorial discretion that resulted in only four prosecutions in the face of 100 reported rapes or sexual assaults.[45]

Commissioner Braceras explained that the Commission has jurisdiction to investigate allegations of discrimination, but not underfunding or a lack of resources. All law enforcement agencies and federal prosecutorial offices are, arguably, underfunded, she said, but this Commission has no authority to influence that debate. She asked panelists and Commission staff to uncover and submit evidence and data that support an allegation of discrimination.[46]

Mr. Bibeau said that on the one hand the United States encourages the tribe to operate as a sovereign nation without federal involvement, and at the same time federal authorities arrest, prosecute, and convict people on the reservation. In the mid 1990s, there were federal convictions of three tribal leaders on two Minnesotan reservations for voting fraud and kickbacks (White Earth Reservation) and theft plus additional charges (Leech Lake Reservation). First, Mr. Pevar said that he and other knowledgeable people passed information to federal investigators for five or six years before the authorities initiated the prosecutions and it seemed to him that nothing was done; second, the Indian communities never learned how their leaders cheated them; although the convictions removed three people, the allegedly corrupt system remained in place; and without an explanation of the offenses, the victims were unable to protect themselves against further crimes or abuses. Furthermore, according to Mr. Bibeau, the Indian people do not know whom to trust.[47]

Commissioner Yaki emphasized the importance of properly allocating resources for the enforcement of civil rights. An examination of the monies allotted to enforcing civil rights statutes is a legitimate question when, for example, an Amnesty International report shows disproportionate rape and sexual assault of Native American women and a lack of prosecution of such cases, Mr. Yaki said. Commissioner Yaki also stated that a 5,000 mile territory that has only one assigned U.S. attorney and one deputy is a civil rights issue regardless of whether or not inadequate resources cause insufficient prosecutions. In the past, Commissioner Yaki asserted, government officials effected injustice and discrimination by assigning weak attorneys to rural minority-populated areas that required extensive travel time to administer justice. Often evidence became stale before authorities could reach a crime scene to collect it. Resources for enforcement are a civil rights issue, Commissioner Yaki concluded.[48]

Commissioners then discussed whether the underfunding of the administration of justice was a civil rights matter. Vice Chair Thernstrom posited that a disparate allocation of resources in law enforcement or prosecutorial offices might have civil rights implications. Commissioner Yaki stated that the role of the Commission on Civil Rights is to determine whether or not the federal government is effectively enforcing civil rights laws.[49]

---

[45] *See id.* at 36–38.

[46] *See id.* at 36-38.

[47] *See id.* at 39-40.

[48] *See id.* at 42-43.

[49] *See id. at* 44–45.

Mr. Pevar said that if the Commission was interested in law enforcement issues, it should seek more experts to speak about racism in that field. He said that other experts would be able to provide factual support for these discrimination claims in law enforcement.[50]

Commissioner Taylor asked Mr. Pevar to explain the remedial plan in *Antoine v. Winner School District*[51] that was submitted. Mr. Pevar explained that it was a massive lawsuit filed in federal court accusing the Winner School District of discriminating against Indian students in discipline and alleging violations of equal protection (a constitutional right) and Title VI of the Civil Rights Act. The plaintiffs engaged in discovery for months, but the case never went to trial. Neither side wanted a trial that would polarize the community. Mr. Pevar explained that the Winner School District's statistics on discipline were clearly supportive of the plaintiffs' position and assisted in bringing the parties to settlement. The federal judge in the case appointed a U.S. magistrate to work with the parties to come up with a remedy. The result, Mr. Pevar said, was a "wonderful" consent decree. Mr. Pevar anticipated that the judge would sign the decree.[52]

Mr. Pevar described several of the consent decree's requirements: First, the school district must hire an Indian ombudsperson to represent the interests of any Indian child in disciplinary hearings with the principal or vice principal. Second, the district must offer several school-wide programs each year that commemorate Indian culture and Indian history. Third, the school must notify parents when their child is involved in frequent disciplinary incidents and offer an opportunity to meet with school officials.[53] Mr. Pevar characterized the plan as (1) stressing the school system's use of informal resolutions for misconduct, although stronger forms of discipline and expulsion are available when other methods fail; and (2) proactive in incorporating Native American culture and seeking to involve the family and community in remedies.[54] Mr. Pevar further reported that the settlement requires the school district to hire a research group to analyze Native American education in South Dakota.[55]

Commissioner Braceras asked Mr. Pevar whether the disciplinary procedures and punishments were the same for white and Native American students. Mr. Pevar responded that they were not — Indian students get an ombudsman and Caucasian students do not, due to the history of discrimination. Commissioner Braceras stated that the same procedures and same processes applying to all students regardless of race are inherent to the mandate of equal protection.[56]

Vice Chair Thernstrom asked what the process was that resulted in the disproportionately high number of disciplinary penalties for Indian students. He stated that school officials conduct a subjective evaluation of the severity of the child's actions, he explained. He alleged that Indian students were charged with graver offenses than white students for identically described conduct. Commissioner Braceras agreed that if the underlying conduct was the same, but school officials cited and punished it differently, then they were discriminating.[57]

---

[50] *See id. at* 48–49.

[51] *See Antoine v. Winner School District* 59-2, 11, No. 06-03007 (D.S.D. Mar. 27, 2006).

[52] *See id.* at 49-51; *Antoine v. Winner School District* 59-2, No. 3:06-cv-03007-CBK (D.S.D. Dec. 10, 2007).

[53] *See id.* at 54; *Antoine v. Winner School District* 59-2, No. 3:06-cv-03007-CBK (D.S.D. Dec. 10, 2007).

[54] *See* Briefing Transcript at 50-51, 54–55.

[55] The text of the settlement is available at http://www.aclu.org/crimjustice/juv/32175lgl20071210.html (last visited Oct. 19, 2009).

[56] *See* Briefing Transcript at 55.

[57] *See id.* at 59–61.

Mr. Pevar described the "disciplinary confession" process in which 95 percent of those disciplined were Indian. He stated that when school officials remove a student from class for a misdeed, they isolate the child until he or she signs a confession, which the principal notarizes and sends to law enforcement. During this time school officials refuse to allow the student to contact his or her parents. The plaintiffs alleged that school staff also denied bathroom breaks to such students and kept them for hours to obtain their confessions. Thus, the disciplinary confessions, Mr. Pevar said, were unreliable as well as discriminatory. Mr. Pevar's suit included the claim that forcing students to write confessions was a violation of the Fifth Amendment protection against self-incrimination. As a result, school officials agreed to stop using this procedure.[58]

Commissioner Taylor asked whether the school district's treatment of incidents of misconduct differed when the teacher or principal was Indian. Mr. Pevar explained that the school district employed only one Indian, but not as a teacher. Thus, the lawsuit also claimed that although there was a high percentage of Indians in the community, the school district had never actively recruited Native Americans. The plaintiffs were unable to obtain information on whether the school districts had received and rejected Native Americans job applications. However, Mr. Pevar reported that the school district was inundated with applications for the ombudsperson position. Thus, when the school district advertised a position it planned to fill with an Indian preference candidate, the outpouring of applications was enormous.[59]

Commissioner Taylor asked how Mr. Pevar described or characterized discrimination when he met with school officials to develop the consent decree. Mr. Pevar said he explained to school officials that he believed they were discriminating against Indians and that he had unequivocal statistics to suggest they were, but he did not want to have to prove it. Furthermore, neither party would gain by going to court. Rather than proving or disputing discrimination, he asked school officials to commit to "doing the right thing in the future" and to adopting procedures that would ensure fairness. Everyone agreed with the recommended procedures, he said, suggesting that perhaps they first must shed their prejudices to reach a resolution in everyone's best interest.[60]

The plaintiffs' statistics, according to Mr. Pevar, "demonstrated that either Indian [students] were more likely to engage in trouble[-making] than non-Indians, or there was racial discrimination." How could you explain, he posed, the fact that 60 percent of the students expelled from school are Indian when only constituting 20 percent of the population? He agreed with Commissioner Braceras that it might be for both reasons. Mr. Pevar then stated that he did not seek to figure that out when meeting with school officials. Rather, he was more concerned with interested parties "doing the right thing."[61]

Vice Chair Thernstrom stated that making it more difficult for the school to remove disciplinary problems interferes with the educational quality of the school. Mr. Pevar said that schools would not have agreed to the settlement if it would tie their hands with respect to discipline.[62]

In response to Commissioner Melendez's question, Mr. Pevar elaborated on the complaint that Native American parents filed with the Office for Civil Rights (OCR) about ten years ago. As a result of OCR's investigation, the school district entered into a settlement agreeing to do more to help Indian students.

[58] *See id.* at 61–62.
[59] *See id.* at 62.
[60] *See id.* at 50, 62-64.
[61] *See id.* at 63.
[62] *See id.* at 64–65.

The school district provided documents that OCR agreed was sufficient to demonstrate compliance. According to Mr. Pevar, OCR closed the case despite receiving a paltry amount of information from the district. The ACLU did a fresh analysis and decided that racial tensions were worse than before OCR had begun its investigation, and filed suit.[63]

Mr. Bibeau added that Native Americans are sometimes denied social services if they live off the reservation. The state has an agreement with the tribal government that Aitkin County residents are eligible for benefits from the Minnesota Family Investment Program (MFIP), but poor tribal members living off the reservation in the jurisdiction are not.[64]

***

Panel Two Discussion

Alvin Windy Boy, Sr.

Mr. Windy Boy reaffirmed the sovereign status of Indian tribes, and explained that the federal government provides health, education, and welfare services to tribes as a result of executive orders, other acts of Congress and treaties with the United States. According to Mr. Windy Boy, this federal trust responsibility forms the basis of providing health, education, and welfare services to tribal people, with numerous court decisions, proclamations, and congressional laws reaffirming this relationship.[65]

He explained that American Indians have long experienced poorer health compared with other Americans, resulting perhaps from their disproportionate poverty, discrimination in the delivery of health services, and cultural differences. American Indians born today have a life expectancy that is 2.4 years less than the non-Indian U.S. population according to Mr. Windy Boy. He claimed that the rates are 600 percent higher for death from tuberculosis; 510 percent higher for alcoholism; 229 percent higher for motor vehicle crashes; 18 percent higher for diabetes; 152 percent higher for unintentional injuries; and 61 percent higher for homicide.[66] He emphasized the particular scourge of alcoholism on Native American families, individuals, and tribal communities.[67]

Mr. Windy Boy noted that such health disparities weaken Native American communities, making them vulnerable. For example, drug dealers view tribal communities, already inundated with alcohol addiction, as easy to infiltrate for drug distribution. Mr. Windy Boy referred to a Mexican drug cartel that targeted Montana and Wyoming tribes near Billings. As reported in national news, the cartel's strategy includes marrying into the tribe, supplying free drug samples to get people addicted, and then forcing addicts to distribute drugs to support their habits. The cartel planned to implement this approach throughout Indian country, Mr. Windy Boy claimed.[68]

---

[63] *See id.* at 67.
[64] *See id.* at 68–69.
[65] *See id.* at 76–77.
[66] *See id.* at 77–78.
[67] *See id.* at 78.
[68] *See id.* at 78–79.

Mr. Windy Boy argued that, given the significant health disparities that tribal people suffer, the federal government should place the highest priority on funding for Indian health care. Many of the diseases that tribal people suffer are treatable or completely preventable given adequate resources and funding. According to him, the federal government has not fully funded American Indians' and Alaska Natives' health services for many years. He noted that over the past 10 years, the medical costs inflation rate averaged 11 percent per year, yet the average annual increase in funding for the Indian Health Services over the same period has been only four percent. He claimed that the Office of Management and Budget usually increases federal agency budgets from two to four percent each year to adjust for inflation; however medical costs inflation rates range from seven to 13 percent. As a result of the underfunding, IHS's tribal health programs absorb the additional costs of inflation, population growth, and payroll increases by reducing health care services. Mr. Windy Boy further claimed that government agencies calculate inflation using a different method than the private sector applies, implying that the latter formula might suggest even greater under-funding. [69]

Mr. Windy Boy reported that no one has investigated questions about whether the level or quality of health care that Native Americans receive in Havre, Montana, differs from that provided to non-Indian patients. He posed questions as to whether hospital staff discriminate against Indians, or lack empathy for Native American patients, or whether the level of care Indians receive differs because of financial factors. He noted that the Indian Health Service's tribal health system has agreements with hospitals to charge Native Americans reduced rates for health care.

Mr. Windy Boy believes his own experience highlights the difference in the health care Native Americans receive from a hospital through the IHS tribal health facility as compared to an individual with private health insurance. Recently, Mr. Windy Boy became covered by private insurance through his wife's employer, Montana State University. In a ranching accident this past spring, he was trampled by a bull and taken to the hospital. When first admitted, he did not have the proof of insurance card; thus the hospital emergency room billed his care to the tribal health facility in Rocky Boy. He underwent tests and x-rays and was admitted for his injuries and released about three days later. Weeks later, after he developed a serious infection, he returned to the emergency room. With his private insurance information entered into the hospital database, he underwent more extensive testing, including a CAT scan, during which medical personnel found he had a broken hip, an injury missed in his first hospitalization. Mr. Windy Boy suggested that the inferior care he received when the institution charged the cost of his care to the reservation's health services is an experience shared by many other tribal people.[70]

Mr. Windy Boy also put forth his view that athletic team names such as the Washington Redskins, the songs and antics associated with team mascots such as that of the Atlanta Braves, and face painting mock Native American ceremonies and are derogatory and discriminatory.[71]

---

[69] *See id.* at 79–80.
[70] *See id.* at 81–83.
[71] *See id.* at 83–84.

Chief James Runnels

Chief Runnels described the City of Farmington's history and also the 1974 event that has resulted in repeated visits from the U.S. Commission on Civil Rights since that time. He also noted that Farmington is an oil and gas center in northwest New Mexico that experiences economic booms every 10 to 15 years, during which the town experiences population growth of 200 to 300 percent. According to him, those who move in during boom times tend to be from out of state. Such persons are frequently unaware of cultural differences with Indians and are unwilling to spend time learning about local issues, he said. Chief Runnels attributed both current and past problems to this huge population influx of those not from the area. Furthermore, he stated that he had seen racial discrimination in Farmington in his more than 20 years there.[72]

As an adjunct faculty member for a local community college, Chief Runnels observed a lack of willingness to incorporate cultural education into school curricula, such as by teaching the Native American style of writing along with the English system. Furthermore, the educational opportunities extended to Native American students do not overcome the barriers of their home lives, including long bus rides to and from class.[73]

According to Chief Runnels, Native Americans encounter difficulties in dealing with the business community in Farmington, some of which lead to police involvement. Farmington businesses' customer service has been generally poor in the past and has given rise to many complaints regarding the way Native American clients are treated, he said. For example, many Native American elders are not fluent in the English language and do not understand the legal payment agreements they have signed to purchase merchandise. When someone arrives to repossess an item for lack of payment, the Native American purchasers often believe themselves to be unfairly treated by both the business community and the police who are called to the dispute. Misunderstanding about repossession is probably one of the most common causes of disputes in Farmington, Chief Runnels asserted.[74]

To help alleviate such problems, the City of Farmington, together with the local Chamber of Commerce, has created a cultural awareness program targeted to the business community. The city government requires all of its employees to go through the program, Chief Runnels noted. He credited the program with addressing difficulties between Native Americans and the business community.[75]

Chief Runnels further reported that the City of Farmington was in the process of establishing a Community Relations Commission in response to a recent report[76] by the U.S. Commission on Civil Rights' New Mexico SAC. Officials had just introduced the resolution to form the body. During the year since Chief Runnels reported on this matter, the Community Relations Commission began meeting monthly and anticipated hearing complaints of discrimination beginning in November 2008.[77] Chief

---

[72] *See id.* at 84–86.

[73] *See id.* at 86.

[74] *See id.* at 86–87.

[75] *See id.* at 90.

[76] *See* NEW MEXICO ADVISORY COMMITTEE, *supra* note 1, at 56.

[77] *See* Briefing Transcript at 90. It has apparently been established, see http://www.navajotimes.com/news/2008/1108/112008racial.php.

Runnels said that the largest change in the City of Farmington is the community's recognition that it needs the Native American population as valued customers to support the city as a retail center.[78]

Chief Runnels stated that the criminal justice system in New Mexico and in San Juan County was discriminatory against minorities. He blamed problems on the poor quality of legal services available to Native Americans, law officers' misconceptions about Native Americans, and police departments' difficulties in recruiting Native American staff, despite vigorous efforts using professional psychologists and an affirmative action plan that is updated every year. He noted that the Farmington Police Department has doubled the number of Indian officers in the last few years, resulting in about twelve Native Americans among 135 officers. [79]

Chief Runnels stated that to combat alcoholism, the city council and the mayor created the Tótah Behavioral Health Unit in the past two years which works towards treatment of the disease instead of relying solely on incarceration to address it.[80]

Chief Runnels noted that overall Farmington has made progress in addressing the concerns of Native Americans, and will continue to do so. City officials have worked successfully with tribal members, including Mr. Yazzie, who also spoke at the briefing.[81]

Barry D. Simpson

Superintendent Barry Simpson described the Bishop, California, school district, which serves 1300 students and is located in a valley along the Sierra Nevada Mountains. Of those, he noted that approximately 20 percent are Native American, 28 percent are Latino, 48 percent are white, and 4 percent represent other groups. The district faces some challenges, according to Mr. Simpson. First, it borders the Paiute Shoshone Indian Reservation, which has approximately 2,000 tribal members. Second, the district is designated as a program improvement school under the guidelines of the No Child Left Behind Act. Third, its schools are experiencing declining enrollment, having lost over 250 students in the past five years. Mr. Simpson explained that the decline results mostly from the locality's increased housing costs, driven up by the proximity of a ski resort. In addition, the area has few opportunities for employment. Despite these challenges, the superintendent characterized his teaching staff as strong, caring, and dedicated to providing a positive environment for all students.[82]

Mr. Simpson described an October 2005 incident on the middle school campus of the Little Bishop School District, which led to a complaint filed with the American Civil Liberties Union. The complaint alleged that the school resource officer acted in a physically threatening manner in an attempt to resolve an issue with a group of Native American students. A second complaint regarding the same incident, alleged that the school district engaged in a pattern of discriminatory discipline. The incident grew out of a young man wearing a headband, which violates school dress code, and escalated quickly. Mr. Simpson explained that he was not superintendent at the time, nor even employed with the school

---

[78] USCCR briefing transcript at 91.

[79] *See* id. at 87.

[80] *See* id. at 90.

[81] *See* id. at 91.

[82] *See* id. at 92.

district. After reviewing the incident, however, he believed that many mistakes were made in resolving the issue. Furthermore, a review of the district's disciplinary data showed that disciplinary actions involving Native American students have occurred at higher frequencies compared to the rates of other student populations, Mr. Simpson said.[83]

Mr. Simpson assumed responsibility for addressing the complaints when he became superintendent of Bishop Union Elementary School District. In September 2008, the district reached an agreement with the ACLU stipulating conditions that, if met, Mr. Simpson claims will improve the district as a whole. The agreement requires ongoing development of staff's cultural awareness and diversity, and the integration of conflict resolution and cultural diversity awareness into students' daily activities. Also, the district will discontinue the school resource officer program, although the school board can vote to reinstate it.[84]

As a result of the agreement, he said that the district is already improving. Disciplinary actions have been reduced. Recent state testing data show that the middle school Native American students exceeded all proficiency targets in mathematics and language arts. Mr. Simpson expressed pride in this academic achievement, a desire to continue improvements, and openness to further strengthening ties between Native Americans and other groups in the school district.[85]

Mr. Simpson stated that he met with Bishop's tribal leaders to ask about their concerns. From the director of the district's Indian Education Center, he learned that Native American parents do not want special treatment for their children, but want their children to behave, to learn, and to be successful. According to Mr. Simpson, the No Child Left Behind Act has had significant effects on the nation's schools, especially in Native American communities. Despite having noble goals, implementation of this Act has been less than perfect. Its desired result of 100 percent proficiency is difficult, if not impossible, to attain. When schools must respond to the demands of high stakes testing, school officials experience greater difficulty in providing a well-rounded curriculum. As school administrators and teachers face mounting pressure to raise test scores, they often sacrifice other curricula, such as the arts, music, and cultural offerings. Under such conditions, schools may force many struggling students to take additional courses in math and language arts and to forego electives, where they may have considerable ability. Mr. Simpson blamed low teacher morale, student and parent frustration, and an increase in dropout rates on the narrowing of curriculum in an effort to raise test scores. He expressed concern that, first, many students, including Native American students, will become increasingly disengaged as programs are slowly eliminated and, more generally, the legislation has some unintended negative consequences.[86]

Finally, Mr. Simpson described what his school district and community had done to improve relations of Native Americans with other groups. First, the school district employs three Native American liaisons who are responsible for better linking the school with home. The liaisons offer academic support before and after school and bring in guest speakers and performers to share Native American culture with all students. The school district offers a Paiute language course. In addition, each year, the school board holds a board meeting at the tribal council chambers on the reservation. This meeting is devoted to discussing the progress of Native American students. School administrators meet regularly with the

---

[83] *See id.* at 93–94.
[84] *See id.* at 94.
[85] *See id.* at 94–95.
[86] *See id.* at 95-97.

Indian Education Parent Committee. These efforts are producing positive results, Mr. Simpson said, but he continues to seek more ways to help strengthen the ties with the Native American community.[87]

Duane H. Yazzie

President Yazzie described the vicious 1974 killings of three Navajo youth and the ensuing Saturday morning marches of 2,000 Native Americans and their supporters protesting Farmington residents' mistreatment of tribal members. The protests, Mr. Yazzi said, were the Navahos' response to decades of discrimination in encounters on the streets and in business transactions, brought to a breaking point by the murders.[88] He then presented current examples of mistreatment.

For example, he relayed a June 2006 beating of a Navajo man by three young whites who used racial slurs as they did so. The victim, Mr. Blackie, survived and the three men received sentences averaging six years each. Authorities relied on the New Mexico hate crime law in extending the length of these sentences. Mr. Yazzi reported that despite Farmington's history of crimes against Navajo people, this was the first time the district attorney filed hate crime charges.[89]

One week after the Blackie beating, a white Farmington police officer shot a young inebriated Navajo, Clint John, four times in the chest and head. Accounts vary on whether Mr. John was armed with the police officer's baton. The area newspaper reported that he was unarmed; however, the San Juan County Sheriff's Department investigated the incident and cleared the officer of any wrongdoing. Mr. Yazzie implied that the investigation was biased, because the sheriff is a former Farmington city police officer, and questioned the standards that allow the Farmington Police Department to use lethal and excessive force against Native Americans. Notably, Mr. Yazzie did not deem the Clint John shooting a hate crime.[90]

Other instances of police misconduct occurred in Farmington in the month after the Clint John killing, Mr. Yazzie alleged. Furthermore, there were reports of several attacks on Native Americans in Cortez, Colorado, another border town, in November 2006. Also, on several occasions in January 2007, armed Forest Service officers harassed and intimidated Native Americans who were offering traditional religious prayers on the San Francisco peaks. According to Mr. Yazzie, the spiritual leaders claim county sheriff deputies detained and interrogated them about their presence at the base of the mountain.[91]

As with the 1974 incidents, Native Americans organized demonstrations following these events, Mr. Yazzie said. For example, on September 1, 2006, Navajos marched on Farmington as a walk for peace and justice. Making the event annual, they conducted another walk in Cortez, in September 2007. Yazzie also noted that in November 2006, Native Americans protested what they view as the history of

---

[87] *See id.* at 97-98.
[88] *See id. at* 98-100.
[89] *See id.* at 100.
[90] *See id.* at 100-101.
[91] *See id.* at 101-102.

discrimination against Native people in Gallup, New Mexico. Mr. Yazzie reported that the Navajo Nation has 13 border towns, each of which has a history of racial mistreatment of Native Americans.[92]

After the recent resurgence of hate crime incidents, Mr. Yazzie reported, the Navajo Nation Council took measures to better document occurrences of hate crimes against Navajo people in towns bordering on the reservation. The Council approved the Navajo Nation Human Rights Commission Act. This act authorized the establishment of a Navajo human rights office to document border town hate crimes against tribal members and to work proactively with local governments and civic groups to minimize or prevent such crimes.[93]

Furthermore, Dinebeiina Nahiilna Be Agha' diit' ahii,(DNA) the Navajo Branch of People's Legal Services, produced a race relations report on the quality of Navajos' lives based on a review of statistical data from the reservation's 13 border towns. Although most adult Navajos have either encountered discrimination firsthand or have heard descriptions of such treatment from family or community members, only two of the border towns that had data responding to DNA's request reported that they had received reports of discrimination or mistreatment of Native Americans, either through hate crimes or police brutality.[94]

Thus, the DNA report explores whether Navajos are victimized in border towns but do not report it. It uses the work of Dr. Barbara Perry of the University of Ontario. Dr. Perry concludes that hate crimes against Native Americans are so widespread that community members consider them normal. She found that in spite of the extensiveness of racial victimization, fewer than five percent of victims report incidents to police. The two main reasons for an unwillingness to report such crimes are: first, the perception that police do not take Native American victimization seriously and, thus, fail to respond appropriately; and, two, the fear of secondary victimization, harassment, or violence at the hands of police officers. The fear of secondary victimization arises from individual and collective experiences and perceptions of police misconduct.[95]

President Yazzie stated that discrimination today appears in fewer instances and in a less aggravated form than what Native Americans experienced in the 1960s and 1970s. At the same time, he argued that it clearly continues. He cited the Federal Bureau of Investigation's 2005 hate crime statistics showing that Alaska Natives and American Indians represent only one percent of the United States population, but are victims of two percent of racially motivated crimes. Mr. Yazzi expressed hope that beatings and killings such as those he described are rare, but suggested that more incidents of deliberate harm to Native Americans may have occurred because of the high numbers of missing people, many of whom disappeared years ago. In addition, he argued that Native Americans continue to be subjected to discrimination in the form of occasional snide racist remarks, outward verbal abuse, and unfair business practices that charge less-educated Navajos excessive interest rates for loans, such as those for purchasing vehicles and mobile homes. Some Native Americans are concerned, he explained, that perpetrators are more adept and refined in their culture of hate.[96]

---

[92] *See id.* at 101–102.
[93] *See id.* at 102–103.
[94] *See id.* at 103. *See also* DNA-People's Legal Services, Inc., Interim Report to the Office of the Speaker of the Navajo Nation Council (Oct. 16, 2006).
[95] *See id. at* 103-104.
[96] *See* Briefing Transcript at 104-105.

Mr. Yazzie acknowledged that the Navajo Nation's limited retail stores and the lack of liquor stores there create opportunities for discrimination and exploitation when Native Americans go to border towns to shop and drink, forcing townspeople to contend with panhandling, inebriated Navajos. He stated that Native Americans perceive that the vast majority of their non-Native neighbors possess good hearts and only a small number exacerbate race problems. Mr. Yazzie further recognized the steps the border town communities of Farmington, Gallup, and Cortez have taken to try to address the scourge of hate crimes and the sustained effort required to change attitudes of entire communities. He indicated a willingness of the Native American community to participate in an enduring work effort.[97]

In closing, Mr. Yazzie praised the Commission on Civil Rights for its scrutiny of the issues. He stated that this attention has encouraged both border towns and the tribal government to seriously consider and address crimes against human rights and dignity.

Panel Two Discussion

Commissioner Melendez asked Mr. Yazzie how to get more accurate reporting of the severity of discrimination in Indian country. If many people fail to report crimes the crime rate is underreported, Commissioner Melendez said. He asked what statistics federal or state agencies should gather. Mr. Yazzie replied that the City of Farmington is trying to establish a process for people to report hate crimes against Native Americans. Furthermore, he has urged Farmington officials to hire complaints-processing staff who the victims would regard as sympathetic. Yet Mr. Yazzi was not optimistic that Farmington and other border towns would develop a mechanism through which Native Americans would volunteer to bring forth issues of discrimination.[98]

Chief Runnels added that Farmington has a Citizens Police Advisory Commission (CPAC), created some years ago to hear complaints against police officers. It is part of the city manager's office, not the police department, but it still struggles with trying to reach the Native American community so that its members are inclined to voluntarily bring complaints before the group. He remarked that some Native Americans attended CPAC meetings to complain about predatory business practices. However, the city manager's office has no jurisdiction over businessmen and CPAC has declined to provide advice about legal matters not within their purview.[99]

Chief Runnels was hopeful that the Navajo Nation's Human Relations Commission would provide a comfortable outlet for Native Americans to complain about discrimination and that this organization would forward matters concerning police misconduct to the CPAC.[100]

Commissioner Melendez then asked whether the police department should hire a Navajo public relations officer to represent the Farmington Police Department in interactions with the Native American community. Chief Runnels replied that the Farmington Police Department had recently hired staff and was considering new positions, such as a public relations officer. Also, the City of Farmington just created a public relations position, according to Runnels. He added that he had not considered a position

---

[97] *See id.* at 105-106.
[98] *See id.* at 107-108.
[99] *See id.* at 111–112.
[100] *See id.* at 111–112.

specifically geared toward the Native American community, but knew of some good candidates for one.[101]

Mr. Yazzie stated that to obtain information about discrimination against Native Americans, he preferred the Navajo Nation's Human Relations Commission, which is inside the Native American community, rather than CPAC or any outside organizations because the process the Navajo Nation is developing to document border town discrimination considers the difficulties in generating those statistics. He asked the Commission to support the Navajo Nation's effort to create a Navajo Nation Human Rights Commission to track such discrimination.[102]

Commissioner Yaki said that many large cities have community relations or human rights commissions that deal with issues such as police misconduct (which people are uncomfortable presenting to police commissions), civil rights, and economic development. He asked the local officials whether they had worked together with, or drawn on the expertise of, other border towns, communities, jurisdictions, states, reservations, or tribes, whether Chippewa, Cree, or Navajo, to identify common concerns and strategies to address them.[103]

Superintendent Simpson said each of the seven school districts in his county borders a reservation. Staff from the various school districts has communicated about starting a Native language class, but his system has engaged in very little coordinated effort to promote better community relations among tribal members and residents of border towns. Mr. Simpson was not aware of any state effort to encourage school districts to work together on such issues.[104]

Reporting on coordination among police departments, Chief Runnels explained that the towns closest to Farmington are Gallup, New Mexico, and Cortez, Colorado. The Farmington Police Department does not consult with officials from Cortez because Colorado's state laws differ from those in New Mexico, especially in law enforcement, he explained. Farmington authorities do have contact with their counterparts in Gallup and frequently with the mayor. Indeed, Farmington's deputy police chief, assistant city manager, and two officers were scheduled to meet with the Gallup mayor and police chief to develop common solutions to shared issues in just a few days, Chief Runnels said.[105]

Mr. Windy Boy said that in response to a report of the U.S. Commission on Civil Rights in 2001,[106] that representatives of three or four reservations in north central Montana (bordering Canada) met on four or five occasions, and included officials from the Commission and the Department of Justice. He stated that the Fort Belknap Indian Reservation developed a plan and had implemented it a year and a half ago. He did not know of any result from this effort.[107]

Commissioner Melendez commented that in 2003, the Commission's Rocky Mountain Regional Director, John Dulles, organized an effort to bring together representatives of border towns in various states to identify the most pressing of their common problems. He urged the Commission to hold such

---

[101] *See id.* at 112–113.
[102] *See id.* at 113-114.
[103] *See id.* at 114–115.
[104] *See id.* at 116.
[105] *See id.* at 116-117.
[106] *See* MONTANA ADVISORY COMMITTEE, *supra* note 2.
[107] *See* Briefing Transcript at 120–121.

regional meetings in the future. Mr. Windy Boy agreed that bringing together people in authority, whether from tribal governments or city or county commissions was a worthwhile project.[108]

Commissioner Melendez asked for an elaboration on the nature of unfair business practices against Native Americans, specifically whether they consisted of higher interest rates or related to language barriers. Chief Runnels stated that, in New Mexico, predatory lending to many people, including Native Americans, has always been an issue. He attributed problems to businesses offering payday loans and the high interest rates they charge. He said in the last legislative session, the State of New Mexico passed a law regulating such enterprises. He added that the person buying an automobile or mobile home often may not read or understand the contract and the caveats contained therein that subject the buyer to legal action. For a long time, Farmington car salesmen allowed the purchaser to drive the car away before checking the buyer's credit for approval of a loan. When the loan was disapproved, the dealer demanded the car back, but charged a usage fee. Mr. Runnels said this procedure is less common now than it used to be, suggesting that business practices have improved today.[109]

Indeed, Mr. Runnels stated that business practices have improved because entrepreneurs now realize that their profit is higher if they treat customers well. New Mexico, he explained, is a gross receipts tax state, drawing little revenue from property taxes. The community's revenues and the means for the city to grow come from sales tax. Therefore, everyone is a valued customer. Mr. Runnels said that, although much smaller, the City of Gallup was getting more business from Native Americans than Farmington. When Farmington city council members and businessmen approached Gallup entrepreneurs about this, they found that Gallup businesses treated their customers better. Thus, Farmington has tried to improve customer service.[110]

Although Mr. Windy Boy supported the notion that both tribal organizations and city or county governments should work together to address racism in border towns, he was less optimistic about whether Native Americans' concerns could be easily resolved. He alleged that the Federal Bureau of Investigation did not follow up on many crimes on the Rocky Boy reservation because the federal government does not recognize the indigenous rights of Native Americans. He stated that the United States (along with other countries that have indigenous people—Canada, Australia, and New Zealand) has not signed a key treaty that would achieve this purpose.[111] Mr. Windy Boy stated that Native American representatives asked Congress to address the rights of indigenous peoples in the Homeland Security Act, but the bill did not include their recommendations regarding Indian country.[112]

The Commissioners discussed whether, because of the broad range of issues emerging from the briefing on discrimination in border towns, the topic merited further attention. Commissioner Yaki suggested bringing people from many jurisdictions, states, and local governments to speak in greater detail on broadly-occurring problems and making full use of the knowledge and work of current and former members of the Commission's state advisory committees. Commissioner Heriot recommended choosing

---

[108] *See id.* at 117-118, 121.
[109] *See id.* at 121–123.
[110] *See id.* at 123-124.
[111] The Declaration on the Rights of Indigenous Peoples was adopted by the United Nations General Assembly in 2007. GA Res 61/178, U.N. Doc. A/61/L.67/Add. 1 (Sept. 13, 2007).
[112] *See* Briefing Transcript at 109-110

a single issue for a focused hearing, then drawing conclusions. Commissioners thanked the panelists for participating in the briefing and concluded the event.[113]

***

---

[113] *See id.* at 125–27.

PANELISTS' WRITTEN STATEMENTS

This part presents the invited panelists' written statements of their intended comments for the briefing. The first panelist to speak at the briefing, Mr. Stephen Pevar, did not provide a written statement. William J. Lawrence, owner and publisher of the *Native American Press/Ojibwe News*, of Bemidji, Minnesota, and an enrolled member of the Red Lake Band of Ojibwe Indians, submitted a written statement.

Statement of Frank Bibeau, Attorney, Anishinabe Legal Services

Forms of Discrimination

My focus as an Impact litigation attorney I focus on institutional discrimination. Here in Minnesota, most reservations tribal members are subject to the *criminal* laws of the state. However, not all laws called criminal by the state are criminal in nature, and may actually be civil for which the state lacks subject matter jurisdiction.

Because governments are working harder to find every penny for their budgets, they do not automatically recognize their lack of jurisdiction and prosecute tribal members and recover fines and costs when they may not actually have the right.

Efforts to Improve

The Bemidji Area Chamber of Commerce has had a Race Relations Task Force for 20 years to help businesses understand how to attract and retain Indian employees. The ACLU has established the Greater Minnesota Racial Justice Program which monitors courts for disparate treatment. Anishinabe Legal Services serves the White Earth, Red Lake and Leech Lake Reservations for civil matters and treaty rights. There is also the Regional Native Public Defender Corp serving tribal members on Leech Lake and White Earth.

Locally, the Chief Judge of the Ninth District Court in Walker, Minnesota has established procedures to identify cases which involve tribal members on the reservation to have the cases transferred to tribal court, before making people drive to state court and spend the day to have the ticket transferred, if they know to ask. ICTV is in the works to have tribal members make first appearances and arraignments done at tribal court to alleviate state court workloads.

How Has Discrimination Changed?

Most people to people discrimination has been reduced, but when natural resources or taxes are at issue, the questions often turn to Indian questions. So people think all Indians get per capita payments from casinos, when the truth is the majority do not.

Barriers and Opportunities

The opportunities are few; money for education, there is major State University in Bemidji and all 3 local reservations have tribal colleges.

The barriers are many with poverty and significant distance between places and jobs. Barriers include drugs, chemical dependency, racism, discrimination, counties *farming Indians* by legal or court processes to keep county employees employed, by charging and collecting fines, placing kids out of homes (CHIPs), etc.

Another barrier is the internal oppression by tribal government towards tribal members which destabilizes tribal members' income and that of adjacent communities who rely on steady Indian employment as well. Similarly, corruption of traditional values and culture by assimilation which is speed up by Indian Gaming.

Statement of Alvin Windy Boy, Sr.: Evidence of Disparate Treatment of Faith-Based Organizations

Good afternoon, Mr. Chairman and Commissioners. My name is Alvin Windy Boy, Sr. and I am an enrolled member of The Chippewa Cree Tribe of Rocky Boy's Reservation in Rocky Boy, Montana, and a citizen of the beautiful State of Montana. I have had the honor to serve as a Tribal Council member for the Chippewa Cree Tribe Business Committee for 12 years with the last four years serving as the Chairman of the Tribe. During my years on the Tribal Council, I served on many Tribal Leader committees that advocated for Indian Healthcare and building a healthy lifestyle for Tribal people. I served for seven years as the Chairman of the Tribal Leaders Diabetes Committee, a committee of Tribal Leadership representing the 12 Indian Health Service Areas that advise the Director of the Indian Health Service (IHS) on diabetes in Indian Country. I served for several years on the IHS Tribal Self Governance Advisory Committee; the last two as one of the Co-Chairmen. I served as the Chairman of the Rocky Boy Health Board, the governing body for the Nah-Tos Health Center, the Chippewa Cree Tribe's health and wellness facility. I served as the Chair of the Montana Wyoming Tribal Leaders Council - Subcommittee on Health. I was recently appointed by the Governor of Montana to the Montana State Grasslands Commission. Currently, I work for the Chippewa Cree Tribe Water Resources Department as the Tribal Historic Preservation Officer. I appreciate this opportunity to address the issues of discrimination. I would like to thank the Commission for the opportunity to testify at this "Briefing on Discrimination against Native Americans in Border Towns".

Before I begin this testimony, I would like to start my reaffirmation of the foundation of the sovereign status of Tribes with a quote from a well respected Quinault Nation Tribal Chairman and friend, the late Joseph DeLaCruz:

> No right is more sacred to a nation, to a people, than the right to freely determine its social, economic, political and cultural future without external interference. The fullest expression of this right occurs when a nation freely governs itself.[1]

The Foundation: Tribes are Sovereign Nations

The overarching principle of Tribal sovereignty is that Tribes are and have always been sovereign nations. Tribes pre-existed the federal Union and draw our right from our original status as sovereigns before European arrival.

---

[1] The late Joseph B. DeLaCruz, former president, Quinault Nation, 1972 – 1993.

The provision of health, education and welfare services to Tribes is a direct result of treaties and executive orders entered into between the United States and Tribes. This federal trust responsibility forms the basis of providing health, education and welfare services to Tribal people. This relationship has been reaffirmed by numerous court decisions, Presidential proclamations, and Congressional laws.

The Situation Today: Access to Healthcare

Racism come in many forms and is often a domino effect of racist attitudes and actions that negatively impact Tribal people. The result of these negative impacts could be defined by "racial and ethnic disparity".

American Indian/Alaska Native Health Disparities

American Indians have long experienced lower health status when compared with other Americans. Disproportionate poverty, discrimination in the delivery of health services and cultural differences has contributed to the lower life expectancy and disproportionate disease burden suffered by American Indians. American Indians born today have a life expectancy that is 2.4 years less than the US All Races.

American Indians die at higher rates than other Americans from:

- Tuberculosis – 600% higher
- Alcoholism – 510% higher
- Motor Vehicle Crashes – 229% higher
- Diabetes – 18% higher
- Unintentional injuries – 152% higher
- Homicide – 61% higher

Some of these health disparities are historic. Alcoholism continues to be a serious challenge to American Indian health. Since its introduction to Tribal people early in this Nation's history, alcohol has done more to destroy Indian individuals, families and Tribal communities than any disease. Today in 2007, Tribal people are dying at a rate 510% *higher* than other Americans from alcoholism. The overall impact of these health disparities has made us "at-risk" communities, weakened and vulnerable. In fact, as reported in the national news, a Billings Area (Tribes within Montana and Wyoming) Tribe was targeted by Mexican drug cartels because of their history with alcoholism. The drug dealers figured that the Tribal community (already inundated in alcohol addiction) would be easy to infiltrate for drug distribution. Their business plan included marrying into the Tribe, giving free samples to get people addicted and then get them to distribute to support their addiction. This approach is being implemented throughout Indian Country.

As the federal government develops models or "best practices" that aim to reduce or eliminate racial and ethnic disparities (i.e. "Closing the Gap") a balance needs to be made between the federal deficit model (comparison to All U.S. Races) and a positive development model. Otherwise health policy (and the subsequent allocation of funding toward Indian healthcare) will be determined on the basis of Tribes being a marginalized minority and not as sovereign nations with distinct treaty rights, which have been negotiated with the *"full faith and honor of the United States of America"*.

Indian Healthcare Funding

Given the significant health disparities that Tribal people suffer, funding for Indian healthcare should be given the highest priority within the federal government. Many of the diseases that Tribal people suffer from are completely preventable and/or treatable with adequate resources and funding.

For some time now, the United States has not funded the true need of health services for AI/AN people. The medical inflationary rate over the past ten years has averaged 11 percent. The average increase for the IHS health services accounts over this same period has been only 4 percent. This means that IHS/Tribal/Urban Indian (I/T/U) health programs are forced to absorb the mandatory costs of inflation, population growth, and pay cost increases by cutting health care services. There simply is no other way for the I/T/U to absorb these costs. The basis for calculating inflation used by government agencies is not consistent with that used by the private sector. OMB uses an increase ranging from 2–4 percent each year to compensate for inflation, when the medical inflationary rates range between 7-13 percent. This discrepancy has seriously diminished the purchasing power of Tribal health programs because medical salaries, pharmaceuticals, medical equipment, and facilities maintenance cost Tribes the same as they do the private sector.

In FY 1984, the IHS health services account received $777 million. In FY 1993, the budget totaled $1.5 billion. Still, thirteen years later, in FY 2006 the budget for health services is $2.7 billion, when, to keep pace with inflation and population growth, this figure should be more than $7.2 billion. This short fall has compounded year after year resulting in a chronically under-funded health system that cannot meet the needs of its people.

Disparity in Level and Quality of Care

The question that has never been investigated in Havre, Montana is do Indians receive different care at the local hospital in comparison to other patients? Are Indians discriminated against by hospital staff and is the level of care provided to Indians different because of financial factors (Indian Health Service/Tribal Health have reduce rate agreements with the hospital), or lack of empathy by hospital staff including assumptions made by staff about Indian patients, i.e. Indians are only in the emergency room to obtain pain pills. I can only speak from my own experience, but I do know that my experience is shared by many other Tribal people.

For the first time in my life, I am covered by private insurance through my wife's employer. I never thought that I would receive different health care from the hospital due to my status as a recipient of healthcare through our IHS "compacted" Tribal health facility. I was hurt this past spring in a ranching accident. My wife had not received her proof of insurance card, although I was covered, so the hospital emergency room billed my care to our Tribal health facility. I was run through the process of tests and x-rays. The doctor I was assigned to was the on-call doctor, a doctor I had never seen before. I was admitted for my injuries and released two days later. I was still in pain and my mobility was limited to crutches and a cane for the next several weeks. Part of my injuries included an abrasion on my leg where layers of skin were gone. Although I followed up care with the same doctor who treated me during my initial hospital stay, I developed an infection serious enough for my wife to insist I return to the emergency room where I was then readmitted for staph infection. This time, however, my private insurance information had been entered into the hospital database. To my amazement, I received a cadre of services that were not offered in the previous stay. One of those tests was a Doppler circulation test where blood pressure cuffs were placed on four parts of my leg to check blood circulation. I was then given a CAT scan of my hip, where it was discovered I had broken a small bone in my hip, explaining the pain and lack of mobility. I asked hospital staff why this wasn't done the first time when I was admitted and the answer was they didn't know they were only doing what they were told. My problems resulting from the injury and lack of care I received at the initial hospital visit still linger. I know I would have never known anything different without this experience of "private insurance." The question remains in my mind; Do Indians receive different care because of their IHS/Tribal health status?

The Situation Today: Access to Justice

Another perception that Indians in the Havre area face is that there is no law enforcement on the reservation. Paul Harvey once said, "If you want to get away with murder, do it in Hays, Montana" a small town located on the Ft. Belknap reservation. In an investigative report by student reporters from University of Montana, local business owners from Havre stated to the undercover reporters that there is no law at Rocky Boy (reservation). At first, as a former Tribal leader, I took offense to such statements. Rocky Boy does have a law and order code, and a small, overworked but competent police force. But the fact is that any major crimes committed on the reservations fall under the jurisdiction of the United States Federal Court system, prosecuted by the U.S. Attorney's Office, investigated by the Federal Bureau of Investigations (FBI). It has long been known that the FBI takes their time investigating crimes that they choose to and failing to follow up on other, serious crimes, like murder and rape.

My nephew was brutally murdered 100 feet from his home in a town site at Rocky Boy. He was murdered in May of 2004 and even today, the FBI has failed to finish the investigation of my nephew's murder. The community knows who killed by nephew, the family has reported to the FBI who it was and provided the FBI with a motive. Instead of justice, my sister has been charged with harassment for talking to the very individuals that murdered her son, while the assailants go free. This scenario is repeated on all reservations in Montana. Interestingly, the U.S. Department of Justice does not publish how many open, unsolved murders and other high crimes cases are on the reservations.

Indians are also prosecuted and persecuted by law enforcement off the reservation. For such a small population in border towns, Indians seem to be able to commit the majority of crimes. Open the Havre Daily News on any given day and read the sheriff's report, 90 percent of the crimes reported were committed by Indian people. Most of the crimes are non-violent offensives such as driving without valid insurance or with expired tags. I guess Indians are easy targets for cops. Pull an Indian driver over for speeding or broken taillight and it is most likely the cop will be able to write three to four additional tickets. For these non-violent crimes, the authorities are more than willing to make criminals of Indian people, some just trying to make it to work at a minimum wage job. However, for serious crimes committed by Indians against Indians in border towns the law enforcement seems to be too busy to investigate or prosecute with much vigor.

Again, I speak from my own experience. My brother-in-law lived in Great Falls, MT in 2000-2004. Great Falls is large city for Montana where many Indian people are able to find work. The Blackfeet, Rocky Boy and Ft. Belkap reservations are all within 130 miles of Great Falls and many Tribal members, unable to get housing on the reservation or find work, make their home in Great Falls. My brother-in-law was violently assaulted in his home by three assailants. My brother lived in public housing and was barely getting by. He knew his assailants and several days after the assault, when a police officer finally investigated, he gave their names in his statement. His assailants were also Indians, living with various family members in public housing around Great Falls. Law enforcement never apprehended the assailants, nor were they ever charged for the violent assault against my brother-in-law. I cannot help but wonder if things would have been different if my brother-in-law were white instead of Indian. I am just thankful that his injuries were not life threatening. Those same individuals that assaulted by brother-in-law in 2000 are in prison today for attempted murder.

What Do We Do? An Action Plan

I did not come here today just to complain and tell stories of the hardships Indians endure because of racism we face every day. Racism is nothing new for my people. It is just a part of life, just like the sun rising and setting every day. Although great strives have been made in addressing racism in America since the 1960s civil rights movement, not much has changed for Indians doing business in small rural border towns. Racism is now dressed in Havre. The signs saying "We Don't Serve Indians" have come down from the window fronts and reside in owners' private offices. The attitudes that Indians are supported by the U.S. Government and have an unfair advantage over non-Indians will not disappear overnight. Tribal leaders, educators and Tribal organizations in Montana have taken the first step in addressing racism in border towns by holding conferences to address the issue. The first annual "Racism in Border Towns" Conference was held on the Blackfeet Reservation this past spring. I encourage the federal government to support such educational conferences in a national education effort. Education and awareness is empowerment. Education is only the first small step, however.

Another initiative I urge the U.S. Civil Rights Commission to support is finding federal funding to support an Indian ombudsman position in border towns. Some metropolitan cities such as Seattle and Denver have created Director of Indian Affairs within the City government. These positions have proven very effective in addressing Indian issues, however small rural border towns do not have the funding or resources to support such a position. The irony is the very towns that cannot afford a dedicated Indian ombudsman are the towns in greatest need of the position. The ombudsman will be the buffer between Indians and business owners, law enforcement, education institutions and state and city agencies. The position will be responsible for education and relationship building efforts in border towns. Most importantly, the position will take complaints from Indians and investigate cases of racism and offer mediation services, providing, finally, a voice for Indians.

I welcome any opportunity to work with the Civil Rights Commission to develop an action plan that will strategically target racism in border towns. Let us together move beyond talking about this issue to addressing racism.

Thank you for your time and attention.

***

Statement of James Runnels, Chief of Police, City of Farmington, New Mexico

The City of Farmington has had a long history with different Native American tribes in its over 100 year history. This relationship has been tenuous at best and violent at its worst. Farmington started as many typical western towns with an economy based on the availability of water and fertile land for agriculture. Farmington's early history was one that was repeated throughout the West with varying relations with Native Americans. There were incidences of violence on both sides as well as stories of cooperative efforts with local residents and tribal members. It was also during this time that the religious community began its missionary efforts in the area. This included the building of several boarding schools in concert with the efforts of the federal government in this arena. Farmington's relationship was fairly mundane with local Native Americans in terms of new influences until the discovery of oil and gas around the turn of the century.

The discovery of oil set the tone for Farmington's existence until the 1980's. Farmington began to experience a cycle of "boom and bust" that shaped its efforts at survival. As with any boom town, Farmington saw a substantial increase in outsiders moving into the area. These new arrivals were mostly ignorant to the cultural differences between the local residents and the Native American population. During the "bust" periods, the newcomers to the area left for new opportunities. This cycle created new populations approximately every ten to fifteen years, with a small population of generational locals. This created tension in a number of areas, often leading to discrimination and abuse of tribal members. This friction came to a tragic climax in 1974 with the brutal slaying of three Native Americans by three Farmington youths. The subsequent outcry and unrest led to the eventual start of Farmington's effort to redeem itself.

This cycle caused city officials to finally look at diversity in its economic ventures in order to avoid the "bust" cycles. This transition started in the early 1980's and has resulted in Farmington becoming the retail hub for over 250,000 people, including the members of four Native American tribes. Due to this shift in philosophy, the makeup of the local population has also changed. The local authorities were quick to realize the economy's reliance on its Native American neighbors and a concerted effort was begun to improve the relationship with these groups as well as to prevent the reoccurrence of past injustices.

There are still examples of discrimination among Native Americans but progress is being made. In the area of education, cultural issues are still a problem with local public education. The American public education system is not very responsive to different cultures and the answer has always been to try and assimilate versus incorporating cultural differences into current curricula. Transportation is also an issue on Native lands. Lengthy bus rides are the norm for students, often ending at a residence without running water or a reliable electricity supply.

Unscrupulous business owners are also still an issue in the Farmington area. Many elderly Native Americans have a poor grasp of the English language and are extremely vulnerable to fraudulent business deals. The issue of pay day loans companies has long been a problem in New Mexico. However, the state legislature is just now taking up the issue.

The criminal justice system has long been a subject of concern in its interactions with Native Americans. With a predominately white work force, the cultural differences, and the lack of understanding about these differences, has created misunderstandings and misconceptions about how and why Native Americans act the way they do in the presence of law enforcement and other officials. The lack of an understanding of the criminal justice system combined with an oftentimes shortage of funds to hire effective legal representation has left many Native Americans at the mercy of the system.

Progress is being made, however. The City of Farmington, under the leaderships of former mayor Tom Taylor and current mayor William Standley, has made a concerted effort to right previous wrongs. The City has annually adopted an Affirmative Action Plan for a number of years and uses this plan in its hiring processes. The City was instrumental in the creation of the Totah Behavioral Authority in an effort to address the local street inebriate concerns. The City also created the "Roof", a seasonal wet shelter built to provide a safe environment for the homeless during the winter months. This project has cut the City's exposure deaths to almost zero. The Farmington Intertribal Indian Organization has been in existence for a number of years and was responsible for the running of the Farmington Indian Center. Like many non-profits, funding became an issue. The City of Farmington came to their aid by absorbing the Indian Center into city government providing a steady revenue source and making the center employees city employees.

The biggest step the City is undertaking is the creation of the Community Relations Commission. The Farmington City Council is currently in the process of adopting a resolution creating this commission. The commission will be composed of nine members selected by the mayor. The membership will be diversified based on ethnicity, age, disability, gender, and occupation. Each member will be required to live within the city limits of Farmington. This commission will be tasked with setting standards for positive community relations dealing with cultural diversity. They will establish a procedure for receiving and reviewing complaints, compliments and feedback that includes fact gathering, seeking legal guidance, acquiring information for investigation of an issue and providing bilingual resources. This commission will provide a long needed resource for Native American and other cultures that are currently at a disadvantage in dealing with the American system. The creation of the commission is the end result of a suggestion made by the United States Civil Rights Commission in its 2004 report on Native American relations in Farmington.

Progress has also been made, and is continuing, in the business community. In a joint effort, the City of Farmington, through the Mayor's Office, and former Navajo Nation Vice-President Marshall Plummer, created the Bridging the Cultures program to educate local business leaders and city employees on how to be more sensitive to the Navajo culture as it relates to employment and customer service. A number of large local businesses have also implemented efforts to provide better services to the local Native American population. The city has also expanded its public transportation system in order to provide better access to the public to local businesses.

The education system has also made advancement in the area of improved relations with Native Americans. San Juan College offers a number of opportunities to Native American students. The College's "Native American Student Recruitment and Retention" plan is an aggressive effort to recruit Native American students. To achieve success with its plan, the College created a Native American studies curriculum and increased its Native American staff. The college has also placed an emphasis on helping Native American students adjust to college life by providing financial aid assistance, orientation programs for parents and students, and peer socialization through the United Tribes Club.

The Farmington Municipal School District has also been active in providing services to its Native American students. Its District Indian Education Committee has been very effective in its oversight of Johnson-O'Malley funds as well as creating curriculum and resource guides for Navajo Culture, Language Arts, and Math instruction. The District also sponsors a weeklong Navajo culture workshop for staff and community members in order to promote awareness and understanding of diversity among its participants. The District partners with Fort Lewis College in Durango, Colorado to assist Native American educational assistants earn college degrees as fully endorsed bilingual teachers.

These are just a few of the efforts that the City of Farmington and its businesses, citizens, and supporters have become involved in an attempt to right some of the wrongs that have been heaped on our Native American citizens. While racism and injustices will continue in Farmington and the entire world, there is an understanding in the Farmington area that the Native American people are an integral and important part of the community and should be afforded the rights and respect that they deserve.

***

Statement of Barry D. Simpson, Superintendent, Bishop Union Elementary School District

I would like to thank the commission members for allowing me the opportunity to take part in this important briefing. I appreciate the chance to hear the other panelist's views on our topic today, as well as finding new ways to strengthen the ties within my community so that we can better serve the students of my district.

I currently serve as the Superintendent of the Bishop Union Elementary School District in Bishop, California. We are a small rural school district located in the beautiful Owens Valley on the Eastern Slope of the Sierra Nevada Mountain Range. Our school district serves approximately 1300 students, of those 1300 students approximately 20% are Native American, 28% are Latino, 48% White, and 4% Other. Our school district boundaries border the Paiute-Shoshone Indian Reservation in Bishop. Our school district is currently identified as a Program Improvement school district under the guidelines of the No Child Left Behind Act. In addition, our schools are experiencing declining enrollment, having lost over 250 students in our district over the last five years. The reasons for this decline are due in large part to increased housing costs and few employment opportunities that exist in our small community. Still, with many difficult challenges facing our school district, I am proud to say that we have a strong teaching staff that is caring and dedicated to providing a positive school environment and quality educational experience to all of our students.

You may be asking what makes this school district significant for this briefing. The answer to that question is that my attendance here today is the direct result of an incident that occurred on our middle school campus in October of 2005. This incident resulted in a complaint being filed with the American Civil Liberties Union. Two years ago, the conduct of our School Resource Officer came into question during an incident that took place on our campus. It was alleged that the School Resource Officer acted in a physical and threatening manner in an attempt to resolve an issue with a group of our Native American students. In addition, a second complaint was filed alleging that our school district had engaged in a pattern of discriminatory discipline. I was not the Superintendent of the district, nor employed by the district at the time of this incident so I do not have any firsthand knowledge of the events that took place that day. However, it is clear to me that many mistakes were made in resolving this issue. It is also clear that following a review of discipline data within our school district, it is true that disciplinary actions involving Native American students have occurred at higher rates when compared to other student populations. These are facts that cannot be denied.

As the new Superintendent of the Bishop Union Elementary School District it became my responsibility to work on this issue, and to that end, I believe that we have had some success. In September, the district reached an agreement with the ACLU. This agreement includes several actions that I believe will make a positive impact on the entire district. Our agreement includes ongoing staff training on cultural awareness and diversity issues, as well as the integration of conflict resolution and cultural diversity awareness into the day-to-day lives of our students. The district has also agreed to discontinue the school resource officer program. While this agreement has only recently been signed, many changes have been taking place at our school district over the past year and I am proud to report that we are seeing many positive results. Disciplinary actions have been reduced and recent state testing data shows that our Native American students at the middle school level (6th through 8th grade) have exceeded all proficiency targets in Mathematics and English Language Arts. I realize that these results are only the first steps on our district's path to improvement, but it is my goal to see this trend continue. I view my presence here today as an opportunity to learn new ways to strengthen the ties between our school and the Native American community.

I would like to take a few moments to briefly address the questions that were included in my invitation to this meeting. First, I must admit it is difficult for me to comment on the forms of discrimination that Native American's face in our border towns. However, I have taken sometime this past week to meet with some of our tribal leaders in Bishop. I asked for input and whether there were any concerns that they would like me to stress. One statement I would like to share came from our Indian Education Center Director, he said, "The parents that I work with want their children to be treated as students, not Indian students. We do not want special treatment, we want our students to behave, we want them to learn, to be successful. Our tribe is diverse, our families do not all act in the same way. Our children are individuals and should be treated as individuals." This, I believe is an important statement, perhaps too much time is spent on deciding how to work with groups of students and not enough time spent on working with the individual child.

To continue, I would like to comment on some of the current issues facing the public education system. It is impossible to discuss the issues facing our Native American students without also discussing the No Child Left Behind Act (NCLB) and the significant impact it has had on our nation's schools, especially those in our rural Native American communities. Although, the goals of the No Child Left behind Act are noble, I think we can all agree that the implementation of NCLB has been far from perfect and its desired result of 100 percent proficiency will be impossible to attain. This may be a discussion for another meeting, but, I could not come to Washington D.C. without voicing my opinion. In an environment where schools are facing the demands of high stakes testing it has become increasingly difficult to provide a well rounded curriculum. School administrators and teachers are faced with mounting pressure to raise test scores often sacrificing other important curriculum including the arts, music or other cultural offerings. In fact, many struggling students are now forced to take additional courses in mathematics or language arts and forgo elective courses where they may have a significant ability. I have seen firsthand, where this has lead to low teacher morale, student and parent frustration, as well as an increase in dropout rates. It is my fear that many students, Native American students included, will become increasingly disengaged as many programs slowly become eliminated. Clearly this legislation has had some unintended negative consequences.

Finally, I would like to highlight a few of the steps that we have taken as a school district to improve relationships with our local Native American community. Our school district employs a three Native American Liaison, whose responsibilities include providing a vital link between school and home. Our liaisons offer before and after school academic support as well as bringing in guest speakers and performers in an effort to share the Native American culture with all students. Each year our School Board holds a board meeting on the reservation at the Tribal Council Chambers. This meeting is devoted to discussing the progress of our Native American students. In addition, our administrators attend regular meetings with the Indian Education Parent Committee. These and other efforts are producing positive results. However, we would very much like to explore additional opportunities to strengthen the relationship between the school and Native American communities. I understand that this process will require a great deal of work and it will not happen quickly, but we are dedicated to this improvement effort.

Once again, I would like to thank the members of the commission for this opportunity and I look forward to learning more about the steps we can take to improve as a school district.

Thank you.

***

Statement of Duane H. Yazzie, President, Shiprock Chapter, Navajo Nation

"Yeigo (with determination), Naas (onward) to Farmington the Selma, Alabama of the Southwest" declared Fred Johnson, our Warrior Leader, as 2000 strong, Natives and Non-Native supporters marched on a beautiful idyllic Saturday morning in the summer of 1974. We marched to protest the mistreatment of our people by the racist minority of this thriving border town across the river from the Navajo Nation. The march, one of seven that we did on successive Saturdays, was our answer to decades of outright discrimination on the streets by regular folks and over-the-counter by conniving and greedy business people. The breaking point of what brought us to the streets of Farmington with pounding drums, our medicine people, our elders and young was the murder of three of our Navajo brethren by three young Anglos engaging in their sport of "Indian Rolling". This is where usually under the influence of booze, drugs or just raw hatred of people of color, young white guys would go cruising the late night streets in search of the right prey, a stranded Indian in need of a ride or a coming-down-off-a-high Indian in need of a drink. With promises of a ride or a drink, the unsuspecting Native is whisked away to Chokecherry Canyon or other similar isolated location, where the young white guys proceed to beat their victims. In the case of the three murdered Navajos, the separate scenes were described by then Sheriff Doug Brown, "the white boys after beating the victims, proceeded to place firecrackers in the ears and anuses of the victims and exploded them, they also burned their genital areas over an open fire. They then took rocks the size of basketballs and slammed them down on the heads of the desperate and pleading Indians to make sure they would die".

That was in the summer of 1974, I am sure that the U.S. Commission on Civil Rights is also interested to hear about our current condition. In June of 2006, William Blackie, a Navajo man hoping to get a ride out of town ended up getting hauled out to Chokecherry Canyon by three young Anglo men. They proceeded to beat him up while barraging him with racial slurs including "you brown nigger". Mr. Blackie survived his ordeal; the three men received sentences averaging six years each, the sentences were enhanced by the New Mexico Hate Crime Law. This was the first time the District Attorney had ever filed hate crime charges, despite Farmington's history of crimes against Navajo people. One week after the Blackie beating, a young inebriated domestic abusing Navajo man was shot point blank four times by a white Farmington police officer. Three shots to the chest, one shot to the head. There remains an equally divided contention whether or not Clint John was armed with the police officer's baton. The Farmington Daily Times, the area newspaper has declared that the "unarmed Navajo man was shot by the white police officer". The officer has been cleared of any wrongdoing by the San Juan County Sheriff Department, the appointed investigating entity. The police officer is a former County Deputy and the Sheriff is a former Farmington City Police Officer. We tend to contend that this might be one of those "good old boy situations". We did not deem the shooting of Clint John a hate crime; we more question the standards that dictate the use of lethal force by the Farmington Police Department.

We marched on Farmington again, this time we termed it a Walk for Peace and Justice, we have made this an annual event. This past September we did our Walk in Cortez, Colorado, another border town where a consistent string of incidents that are termed crimes of hate continue to be reported. The Navajo Nation has thirteen border towns and every single one has a history of racial mistreatment of Native Americans.

In the month after the Clint John killing, other examples of police misconduct in Farmington were reported and several separate attacks on Native Americans in Cortez throughout November 2006. And, as recent as January 2007, there were incidents of harassment and intimidation by armed Forest Service officers against Native individuals offering traditional religious prayers on the San Francisco Peaks. The individuals say they were detained at the base of the mountain by County Sheriff Deputies and interrogated about what they were doing on the mountain.

After the recent resurgence of hate crime situations, the Navajo Nation Council took measures to document the incidence of hate crimes against Navajo people in the border towns. The Navajo Nation Council approved the Navajo Nation Human Rights Commission Act, the Act authorized the Navajo Nation to establish the Navajo Human Rights Office; this office is to work proactively to document border town hate crime against Tribal members and also to work proactively with the border town governments and civic groups to minimize such crimes, if not to prevent them. DNA, the Navajo branch of the People Legal Aid Service produced a report called "Race Relations Report"; I submit a copy of the report for the record.

The Report reviewed statistical government data from the thirteen border towns about the quality of life of Navajo individuals. Although we know there are few adult Navajos who have not either encountered such treatment first hand or have heard descriptions of such mistreatment directly from family or community members who have been victimized in one way or another, of the border towns that provided information in response to the data requests, only two (2) reported that they had received reports of any discrimination or mistreatment of Native Americans either through hate crimes or police brutality. Thus, we questioned: Is it possible that Navajos are victimized in the border towns but they simply don't report it? If so, why is that? To answer this question, the Report cites the study of Dr. Barbara Perry, entitled "*In the Name Of Hate: Understanding Hate Crime and A Crime By Any Other Name: The Semantics of "Hate*." Dr. Perry holds a Ph.D. in Sociology from Carleton University, Ottawa, Canada. Her study provides a substantive and detailed analysis in her findings on hate crimes, summarized as follows:

Hate crime against Native Americans is so widespread as to be considered normative by community members. In spite of the extensiveness of racial victimization, fewer than five percent (5%) of victims report incidents to police. The two main reasons given for their unwillingness to report were:

The perception that police do not take Native American victimization seriously and thus fail to respond appropriately.

The fear of secondary victimization-harassment or violence at the hands of police officers, the fear of secondary victimization arises from individual and collective experiences and perceptions of police misconduct.

The forms of discrimination that our people continue to be subjected to, include occasional snide remarks and outward verbal abuse, cheating less formally educated Navajos by charging excessive interest rates in contracts for loans particularly with used cars and mobile homes. The graphic situations that I shared with you earlier are hopefully incidents far and between, however we do have numbers of people who are reported missing; some have been missing for years and there is speculation that some of these individuals may have fallen prey to those that would do us deliberate harm.

The common forms of discrimination we see today appear to be less aggravated and fewer in number than what we experienced in the 1960's into the 1970's, even so some have surmised that perhaps this suggests the perpetrators have only become more adept and have more refined their culture of hate. Even as this appears to be the situation in the Four Corners region, the Federal Bureau of Investigation's 2005 statistics on hate crimes reports that, while "Alaskan Natives and American Indians represent only one percent (1%) of the United States population, they are victims of two percent (2%) of racially-motivated hate crimes".

To their credit, the border town communities of Farmington, Gallup, New Mexico, and Cortez, Colorado have taken definitive steps to attempt to address the scourge of hate crime, we Natives participate in these efforts; we patiently await the outcome of the efforts. We accept that definitive and lasting results are dependent on attitude change of entire communities and as such, these efforts will take sustained and patient work. Much of the reason why opportunity arises for discrimination is economic, in that the Navajo Nation has a limited retail economy; this condition compels us to have to go the border towns to shop. Another cause is that our Reservation is dry and those that unfortunately need to drink are also forced to go where the booze is. This results in a situation where the border towns have to contend with panhandling inebriated street people, thus to a certain measure we bring the problems of abuse through discrimination and exploitation upon ourselves. We do openly submit that we recognize the vast majority of these of our Non-Native neighbors are people with good hearts and that the race problems are exacerbated by a small redneck and/or white supremacist minority.

The diligent scrutiny that the U.S. Commission on Civil Rights maintains on such situations certainly have a positive impact by bringing pressure on the border towns and our Tribal governments to take crimes against human rights and human dignity seriously and that it is an issue important enough to continue to address. We realize that unfortunately racial hate crime is a phenomenon that has always been with humankind and probably will always be with humankind, but as my Dad once told me "just because you know a situation is going to be, don't just let it be, do something".

Thank you for this tremendous opportunity.

***

WRITTEN STATEMENT OF WILLIAM J. LAWRENCE: DISCRIMINATION AGAINST NATIVE AMERICANS IN BORDER TOWNS—A U.S. COMMISSION ON CIVIL RIGHTS INQUIRY

(**William J. Lawrence,** who was invited but unable to attend the Commission's briefing, is an enrolled member of the Red Lake Band of Ojibwe in Minnesota and the owner and publisher of the *Native American Press/Ojibwe News,* which he has operated for 19 ½ years. Mr. Lawrence is proud of running a free press—an independently owned newspaper published for the Indian people—to reveal information that tribal officials often suppress. The newspaper's investigative reporting, he claims, has helped send nine major tribal officials to federal prison for financially scamming their fellow tribal members. Aside from the newspaper, Mr. Lawrence has spent about forty years working in Indian affairs at Red Lake in Minnesota and on behalf of the Colorado River and Mojave tribes in Arizona. He was also employed in contract negotiations for eight years.)

Greetings: I am William J. Lawrence, owner/publisher of the *Native American Press/Ojibwe News*, published in Bemidji, Minnesota. I am an enrolled member of the Red Lake Band of Ojibwe Indians.

I was pleased to receive an invitation to appear before you, however, it was not possible for me to attend in person. Therefore, I am submitting this testimony for your consideration and inclusion in your final report.

Discrimination against Indian people does exist in our local communities. A recent example is the *Minneapolis Star Tribune* article, dated October 29, 2007, detailing how Tom Bernard and Terri Traen, his on-air partner, at KQRS radio—a top rated talk program--were criticized for their anti-Indian comments. They referenced genetics and incest in reference to suicide rates "up there" at Red Lake Reservation. The station apologized for their behavior after Indian leaders protested. The station has also promised to "hire Indian interns and invite members of the Red Lake Chippewa and the Shakopee Mdewakanton communities to be on Barnard's show."

Bernard's discriminatory comments have not been exclusively reserved for the Native American community. He has also been chided for inappropriate remarks directed toward the Somali and the Hmong peoples.

Fortunately, today, this type of behavior is increasingly being challenged and much of the population considers it unacceptable.

There are local efforts at conscientiously combating discrimination. Bemidji has had a Human Rights Commission for 40 years. The American Civil Liberties Union is also active in our community, focusing most recently on racial profiling and court monitoring.

Our local law enforcement leaders and officers appear to be guided by fairness and act under the constraints of civil rights protections and guarantees. They are sensitive to native issues.

Much of what is perceived today as discrimination, i.e., increased numbers of traffic 'stops' for reckless driving, 'pick ups' for public drunkenness, shoplifting, or violent outbursts, as well as higher than average numbers of Natives in jails, is the result of a peculiar kind of ignorance.

But, before we look at that, here's a list of possible reasons why the greater community might see Indians in an unfavorable light:

- Drunken Indian stereotyping. It is illegal to consumer alcohol on many reservations. Natives therefore drive into towns to buy and consume alcohol. Hence their behavior is often blatantly open to public scrutiny.

- Dysfunctional tribal governments – open corruption, mismanagement of resources, lack of accountability, lack of open meetings. Frequent violation of members' civil rights, no checks and balances assuring due process and equal treatment under the law. Tribal Councils have free rein to do whatever they please. Councils control tribal courts and police departments.

- Native Americans are seen as wards of the federal government, as a nation of welfare users, i.e., Government Issue Indians.

- Economic discrimination – Despite owning casinos, reservation Indians do not pay state or most local taxes. Members of the outside community see Indians receiving all kinds of grant monies on a regular basis. They are aware that Indians receive free medical services and free schooling for their children.

- Increasing awareness on the part of the general public of the unfavorable cost to benefit ratio of Indian casinos. For every $1 of profit, there are $3 in related social costs, which are borne by the host community, which is frequently not the Indian community.

- Indians have more hunting and fishing privileges than do non-Indians. This is a source of annoyance for many sportsmen, landowners and farmers.

- When Indians move into towns from reservations they don't always have neighborly and community skills.

- Common ownership of land and resources doesn't teach the pride and the responsibilities of individual ownership. Land and property cost nothing to the reservation residents, and therefore it is not valued or respected.

- Indians are responsible for a high incidence of the crime in the area. Local jails seem to have a high Indian prisoner population.

- Indian populations exhibit high drug use rates, high alcohol and tobacco use. They make other poor life style choices that affect their well being and that of those around them. Their activities often result in high medical costs for everything from increased incidence of diabetes and heart disease to helicopter transport of injured individuals from reservation to medical centers. These trips are most often related to violence due to alcohol/drug use and trafficking, and the taxpayers foot these bills.

- Welfare rates are high in the area, particularly in regard to foster child care placements and child protective services. Currently there is a conflict between Beltrami County and the Red Lake Band of Chippewa over payment of child protective costs.

- Problems with the Educational system are highly evident – low school attendance, low test scores, low graduation rates coupled with high drop out rates, in spite of Indian schools often receiving larger than average per pupil payments. Large numbers of students are bused into Bemidji area schools from the Red Lake reservation. Many Indian kids drop out of school and end up in the drug trafficking business.

- Social problems are worsening. Problems associated with broken families, with too many children being raised by grandparents are evident.

- Credit and finance issues are a problem on some reservations. Banks cannot repossess cars or other assets when a loan is in default.

- Because of increasing social problems on reservations, increasing numbers of Indian people are moving off reservations to cities like Bemidji.

- Money is not an answer to the problem. The federal government budget allocation for Indian affairs this fiscal year was $12 billion. Profits from tribal casinos add another $12 billion (net) to the pot. These dollar figures are divided up among the 500,000-600,000 Native individuals who reside on reservations throughout the U.S. This results in an astonishing per capita figure. Generally, those who do not live on reservations do not share in these dollars.

It is well to observe that there are more non-Indians living on reservations today than there are Indians. And only about 20 percent of the total Native population (excepting the Navajo nation) now resides on reservations. This situation puts non-Indians at peril of civil rights violations by tribal governments, under the concept of Tribal Sovereignty.

This list illustrates some of the reasons area residents may experience a sense of resentment against the Indian population, although overt racism does not seem to be prominent. Such a list can only be presented by a Native American or it is immediately branded as 'racist.' Even so, though I am an enrolled member of the Red Lake Band of Chippewa Indians, I will be branded 'anti-Indian' for printing this.

The list is meant to give just some of the reasons a discriminatory attitude might exist. It is not intended as a justification, merely an explanation.

There are reasons why Native Americans are failing in the educational system and are finding their names frequently spelled out on police blotters and why they find themselves doing jail time.

What we are seeing today is different from what I observed when I was a boy growing up Indian in a white community. At that time there were maybe half a dozen Indian families living in Bemidji. Today, Indians represent about one fourth of the total population figure for the city.

Discrimination of all kinds, over all ages, is based on ignorance—ignorance of the inherent value of fellow human beings. Discrimination is not now, as it was in days past, an excuse to ostracize Indians, largely just because they are different, from the rest of the community.

The problem we are facing today is primarily an ignorance of what is causing the behavior we can readily observe. And this ignorance is purposely kept hidden. The problem is unacknowledged, not-owned-up-to. It is Fetal Alcohol Spectrum Disorder (FASD).

According to figures published by an earlier U.S. Commission on Civil Rights Report, Native Americans are 770 times more likely to die of alcoholism than is the general population. Indians are approximately 500 times more likely to die of accident or injury. The rate of alcoholism among Indians, according to the Indian Health Service, is 627 times that of the national average.

With those statistics, how could the problems of chaos and dysfunction on Indian reservations possibly be caused by anything other than fetal alcohol spectrum disorders? The disorder, I believe, accounts as well for the behavioral issues manifesting in arrests and incarcerations in border towns.

It is also the single biggest factor in the failure of the educational system as it relates to Native children.

Tom Robertson, of Minnesota Public Radio, recently aired a piece entitled "Alcohol exposure affects generations on Indian reservations." The first line of the article asserts, "It's no secret that alcohol has had a devastating impact on American Indians." He follows that statement with, "But what many are less comfortable talking about is the damage caused when pregnant women drink alcohol. Some call fetal alcohol exposure the Number One problem in Indian Country."

In multiple articles over the past year, we've presented voluminous information that supports that assertion. It is my belief that there is not a more serious issue confronting Indian peoples than FASD.

Robertson interviewed a number of individuals associated with the Red Lake, Leech Lake and White Earth reservations in Minnesota.

Sandra Parsons, director of Family and Children's Services for the Red Lake Band of Ojibwe, mentioned that she thinks "people would be literally amazed at how prevalent it might be."

Parsons, who has worked in a variety of positions for many years with Native children, says, in spite of the fact that her agency worked with more than 900 children (out of a population of 5000) last year, at best, acknowledgement of the extent of fetal alcohol damage in tribal communities is "scattershot."

She believes that "fetal alcohol damage" is "the root cause" of the "looming social problems on reservations." Yet FASD remains "one of those hush-hush topics. . . ."

A reservation mother of 3 adopted children told Robertson that her 16 year old daughter has not yet been diagnosed, even though her biological brother received a diagnosis at age 3 and the mother of all 3 of the children admitted that she had drunk heavily during every pregnancy. Without a diagnosis a child is not eligible for intervention services. The child's future is indeed bleak without meaningful intervention.

She says the schools have been "mostly unresponsive," and that there is "very little support in the Red Lake community for her kids' special needs."

Robertson reported that "the number of kids in special education is double the national average. American Indian kids are three times as likely as other kids to drop out of school. In Minnesota, Indians are 12 times more likely to end up in prison."

In my own research I too found that the education system was largely unresponsive. What little I could find out was that, in general, children with FASD are simply lumped into the general category of "learning disabled." This assumption was supported by staff at the Minnesota Organization of Fetal Alcohol Syndrome.

Not to identify children as FASD is entirely inappropriate since each one is as unique as its own fingerprints. The level of impairment in each child will be different, resulting as it does from the innumerable variables associated with in utero development, the age, the behavior and condition of its mother, the amount and times when alcohol was consumed, etc.

Additionally, although the Minnesota Department of Education maintains a 'mum' attitude, it has been established that the number both of alternative schools and students has greatly increased in the past ten years. Children with behavioral problems are often referred to alternative schools.

At the Leech Lake Reservation, Public Health Nurse Mary May works to educate women regarding the dangers of drinking while they are pregnant, but says, "alcohol. . . is so ingrained into the fiber of many tribal families, education isn't always enough."

She continues, "there's just an incredible level of denial about alcohol affecting babies and I am not sure how to break through that denial." She adds, "addiction makes it difficult to stop fetal alcohol damage."

Leech Lake Tribal Judge Anita Fineday "suspects fetal alcohol damage is behind much of the family dysfunction. She adds, "My guess is that 90 percent of those cases include a parent or a grandparent who has fetal alcohol effect or syndrome."

This means of course that FAS is two to three generations deep. "Brain damaged parents and grandparents are trying to raise brain damaged kids. . . ."

A Bemidji pediatrician confirms that opinion. He told us that it is not unusual for him to deliver a third generation FAS baby.

Judge Fineday sees a connection between alcohol and the poverty found on reservations. She said young women have lost all sense of hope, either for themselves or for their babies.

The poverty that is ubiquitous on reservations is doubly hard for the people to bear when they see their duly elected tribal officials paying themselves salaries of more than $100,000 a year in counties where the average per capita income is $10,000 a year.

At White Earth reservation there are approximately 350 new child protection cases in tribal court. This figure does not include cases heard in state court.

Allan DeGroat, Director of a five-year grant to combat FAS says, "Changing the mind set of the community is a huge challenge."

Recognizing that diagnosis is essential to the provision of meaningful interventions for FAS affected individuals, his over-all goal is to create a reservation-wide diagnostic clinic during the next year. This will go a long way toward helping FAS victims.

Indian communities assert they are not alone in this problem. They are right of course. But the fact remains that FAS has a greater presence and influence in small, isolated/exclusive ethnic communities, where poverty is an ongoing condition.

The incidence, especially for Native Americans, is far greater than anyone believes. The situation remains unacknowledged by tribal officials (including Indian health services), law enforcement agencies, the justice system, the penal system, and the public schools system.

It is the number one cause of mental retardation in this country. Sixty percent of persons affected by fetal brain damage end up in trouble with the legal system. Fifty percent of that number end up in court and 30 percent of that number end up in prison.

Fifty to eighty percent of school children in some reservation schools are affected. The figure rises as high as 100 percent of the school population in isolated Alaskan villages. The percentage of children in public schools with FASD remains undiscovered/undisclosed.

These figures indicate, in part, the enormity of the problem. They do not however convey the intense personal suffering that those who are its victims experience, nor does it give any idea of the severe, debilitating effects experienced by caregivers and family members. It is at the heart of every problem on every reservation in this country. It is responsible for poverty; discrimination; family, societal and tribal governmental dysfunction; social and domestic violence; crime, drug and alcohol problems. It has gone unowned for far too long.

Those persons, including entities of the U.S. government, who want to change conditions for the better for individuals on Indian reservations must address themselves to this problem before progress can be made in the areas of poverty, unemployment, economic development, education, self-sufficiency, or in any other critical area.

The best place to start, in my view, is with law enforcement agencies and the public school system. In order for any progressive change to take place, policy makers and the tax paying public need to see the enormity of the problem.

Law enforcement agencies and the judicial system could do great good by assessing and recording the incidence of fetal alcohol damage in those who are apprehended for misbehavior and/or who appear before the court.

This is one sure way to give the public a view of the scope of the problem and an understanding of the cost associated with FASD individuals and the law. It is appropriate since so many individuals affected with FASD get into trouble with the law.

Although it would take time, proper identification of FAS individuals and proper intervention could help ease the problem of strained court resources, overcrowded dockets and jails.

The public school system is the next most obvious institution to be brought into line on attacking this issue. Increasing numbers of children with behavioral problems are showing up in schools. If unidentified by age 12, the likelihood is great that the child will end up incorrigible and terribly vulnerable to exploitation. If however a child is diagnosed by age six, its chances for a more normal life, with limited behavioral issues, are great. Interventions are most successful when they start early and continue uninterruptedly. Such intervention is essential.

Children with FAS impairments, who bumble through life without the benefit of diagnosis and intervention—and the numbers are very great—often become the foils of drug dealers, the 'fall guys' for gangs, and the perpetrators of violence and crime. But, most importantly, they become the victims of all of the above.

School is where change needed will have to happen. Society created schools in order to produce productive, self-sufficient, contributing members. After all, a child spends more time at school than s/he does at home. They already have in place many of the resources needed to help. Furthermore schools have a vested interest in successfully managing children with behavioral issues. What they don't have is a mission, a mandate. We should give it to them.

It's a huge and difficult problem to deal with as it involves blame and stigma. It grew out of poverty and despair. It involves deep seated familial and societal practices. Drug/ alcohol addictions and illicit traffic are side effects. Federal and state governments will need to support correctional efforts with dollars and expertise.

There is only one ray of light in the whole scenario. According to University of Washington experts on the subject, fetal alcohol syndrome is not genetically transmitted. That means individuals with fetal alcohol damage, provided they do not consume alcohol during their pregnancy, will not pass their impairment on to their children. This also means, with concerted effort and persistent work, fetal alcohol problems can be and must be overcome in the long run.

.....

Sometimes I flinch and would like to turn away from the on-going despair that haunts almost every Indian reservation I've seen. My attached testimony will hopefully open some eyes to at least one explanation for this terrible situation.

There is much that is wrong in Indian Country. It is questionable even whether or not Indian Country has a life expectancy of anything more than a comparatively few years. Civil rights violations and corruption by elected and appointed tribal officials is endemic. Reservations are in danger of imploding, scattering the little parts into the winds.

Nothing short of monumental effort can reverse the situation.

To that end, I congratulate the Commission for its work thus far on Native American issues and respectfully suggest several areas that warrant your scrutiny in future projects. They are:

1. An analysis of federal Indian policy, the damage it has created among Indian peoples and suggestions for repair of the system. Chameleon-like, federal Indian policy has wavered between extermination/assimilation and guilt; paternalism and Indian self-determination, and has made it possible for an elite few to rob their constituents via Indian gambling. It has created a dependent population, and is responsible for the on-going poverty of reservation Indians.

2. An examination of Indian Tribal Sovereignty. Continued subjugation of Indian peoples is not being done by the dominant culture. Rather it is Indians perpetrating outrages against their fellow Indians. Under the protection of Tribal Sovereignty, tribal governments deny their tribal members the ordinary rights of American citizenship. Reservations are administered by policy makers who are not subject to the checks and balances of a democratic government. They do not function under the rule of law.

3. A study of the costs to benefits that result from Indian gambling and recommendations for beefed up regulations and greater accountability. Tribes successfully withhold financial information about their casino operations, even from their own members. Tribal officials have easy access to the huge sums of cash the casinos bring in, and there is little to keep them from benefiting illegally from this access.

Tribal members do not share equally in the cash benefits from a casino.

Additionally, many of the studies that have been done regarding the benefits of casinos have been done by those with vested interests. Academic studies indicate that the presence of a casino in an environment attracts and increases violent and other forms of crime. They also suggest that for every $1 of benefit, there is an accompanying social cost of $3.

***

APPENDIX A: PANELIST BIOGRAPHIES

Stephen Pevar, Hartford, Connecticut, authored *The Rights of Indians and Tribes,*[1] a seminal work representing one of his specialty areas for litigation and lecturing. Mr. Pevar has litigated some 200 federal cases involving constitutional rights in more than ten Federal District Courts, three different U.S. Courts of Appeals, and the U.S. Supreme Court. His expertise also extends to free speech, prisoners' rights, and separation of church and state.

Mr. Pevar graduated from Princeton University in 1968 and the University of Virginia, School of Law, in 1971. From 1971 through 1974, he was a staff attorney with South Dakota Legal Services on the Rosebud Sioux Indian Reservation. From 1976 to the present, he has served as national staff counsel for the American Civil Liberties Union. In addition, from 1983 to 1999, Mr. Pevar acted as adjunct professor at the University of Denver, School of Law, where he taught a course on federal Indian law.

Frank Bibeau, Cass Lake, Minnesota, is an attorney for Anishinabe Legal Services serving White Earth, Leech Lake, and Red Lake Reservations in northern Minnesota. He focuses primarily on litigation in Indian Country and presently has four cases before the Minnesota Court of Appeals addressing different Indian civil and treaty rights. Mr. Bibeau is an enrolled member of the White Earth reservation and has resided on the Leech Lake reservation for the past 25 years.

Mr. Bibeau's legal work includes several years in private practice and some—from 2001 to 2004—as a tribal attorney for the Leech Lake Reservation. He also spent more than a decade working closely with another expert, William Lawrence, to write and report, through *the Native American Press/Ojibwe News,* on tribal members' rights and civil rights both on and off reservations in Minnesota. Prior to becoming an attorney, Mr. Bibeau served the State of Minnesota in several capacities over a 15-year period, which included educating the Minnesota Legislature for five sessions in the late 1980s.

Alvin Windy Boy Sr., Box Elder, Montana, is an enrolled member of the Chippewa Cree Tribe in Box Elder, Montana. He has served on the Chippewa Cree Tribal Council for the past four consecutive terms. In the past, Mr. Windy Boy has served his own tribe and the tribes in the States of Montana and Wyoming and the nation in many capacities, many of them health related. He acted as chairman on the Rocky Boy Health Board for ten years and the Montana Wyoming Area Indian Health Board for eight years. He has served on the National Indian Health Board and the National Tribal Self-Governance Advisory Committee. He chaired the National Indian Diabetes Initiative Workgroup and actively participates in other such groups. With his eye constantly on legislation that may affect Indian people, Mr. Windy Boy has tirelessly conveyed concerns to United States congressmen and the many subcommittees that affect Indian country and the services they receive. Mr. Windy Boy has met with the President on many occasions and continues his advocacy for Indian people at a pace unmatched by his peers.

In addition to public service in the political arena and the health field, Mr. Windy Boy is an active participant in his traditional ceremonies and continues to dedicate his life to learn, teach, and practice the traditions of his father and grandfathers before him. He strives to be an honorable warrior using his love

---

[1] See Steven Pevar, *The Rights of Indians and Tribes* (Southern Illinois University Press, 2002) or a later publication by the same title (New York University Press, 2004). Also see the young-adult version of the same book entitled *The Rights of American Indians and Their Tribes* (Puffin, 1997).

of his people and their ways as guidance for living and promoting Indian issues. He bears responsibility on behalf of many friends and colleagues throughout the nation to continually remind Congress, with his presence, that Indian people are alive and that tribes are still an integral part of this nation.

Mr. Windy Boy's father was tribal chairman and tribal council for 24 consecutive years. His mother was a member of the Assiniboine Tribe from Fort Belknap. Alvin and his siblings were raised traditionally and continue to practice their ceremonies—participating in weekly family sweats and praying as a family unit. In addition to raising fine horses and cattle, Alvin is a renowned fancy dancer and singer. The Windy Boy family participates in the pow-wow circuit each summer, a time of getting together and meeting old friends and relatives.

Chief Jim Runnels, Farmington, New Mexico, has been with the Farmington, NM, Police Department for over 21 years. A native of Fort Worth, Texas, he relocated to Farmington in December 1979. Chief Runnels started his career in Farmington as a patrol officer and assumed many positions while working his way through the ranks. He held every supervisory rank within the department and was appointed Chief in December 2006. Prior to his time with the Farmington Police Department, Chief Runnels spent ten years with the Fort Worth, Texas, Police Department starting as a police cadet and serving as a patrol officer and investigator.

Chief Runnels graduated from the University of Texas-Arlington with a Bachelor's of Science in criminal justice and the University of Colorado with a master's degree in political science. He is a graduate of the 207th session of the FBI National Academy, the FBI Southwest Command College, and the Northwestern University Traffic Institute School of Police Staff and Command. Chief Runnels has served on a number of local boards including the San Juan County Domestic Violence Task Force, the Farmington Family Crisis Center, San Juan Catholic Charities, Four Winds Recovery Center, and Presbyterian Medical Services Neighborhood Advisory Council. He is also an adjunct faculty member at San Juan College, teaching in the Political Science and Criminal Justice departments.

Barry D. Simpson, Independence, California, currently serves as the superintendent of Bishop Union Elementary School District in Bishop, California. He served as superintendent in two previous California systems—the Sausalito Elementary School District and the Round Valley Joint Elementary School District. Mr. Simpson received a Bachelor's of Arts in economics from Whittier College and a Master of Arts in education from Chapman University. He is currently a doctoral candidate at the University of LaVerne. Mr. Simpson began his education career as an elementary school teacher in the diverse community of Delano, California, and now proudly serves as superintendent of the district that he attended as a young student.

Duane H. Yazzie, Shiprock, New Mexico, is a leading Navajo advocate against the abuses of civil rights and human rights. Currently, he presides as president of the Shiprock Chapter, New Mexico, the largest local government unit of the Navajo Nation. Indeed, Mr. Yazzie has been in public service for 32 years, mostly on behalf of the Shiprock community. He was elected to two terms, in 1988 and 1992, on the Navajo Tribal Council. Before that, he was executive staff to the Council's chairman and vice chair. Mr. Yazzie also sat on the New Mexico Human Rights Commission for six years and has long served as a consultant, work he has continued into the present.

Mr. Yazzie is self educated with computer programming training and completed coursework at the Navajo Community College. He has been an activist since the late 1960s, having taken public positions against unmitigated exploitation of natural resources, abuse of workers by big industry and corrupt tribal governmental practices.

APPENDIX B: LIST OF PUBLIC COMMENTS AND DOCUMENTS

Research Report

- DNA-People's Legal Services, Inc., *Race Relations Report,* Final Report to the Office of the Speaker of the Navajo Nation Council, Apr. 16, 2007.

Court Documents

- State of Minnesota Supreme Court, *Buddie Greene, Petitioner/Appellant, v. Commissioner of the Minnesota Department of Human Services and Aitkin County Health and Human Services,* Respondents/Appellees, No. A06-804, Appellant's Reply Brief, Anishinabe Legal Services, Frank Bibeau, Esq., Megan Treuer, Esq., attorneys for petitioner; Lori Swanson, Attorney General, State of Minnesota, Margaret Chutich, Assistant Attorney General, James Ratz, Aitkin County Attorney, attorneys for respondents, Nov. 19, 2007.[1]

- State of Minnesota Court of Appeals, *Fred Morgan, Jr., Appellant, v. 2000 Volkswagon, White Earth License No. 279, VIN #3VWRA29M2YM125643,* Respondents, No. 07-1922, Appellant's Brief and Appendix, Anishinabe Legal Services, Frank Bibeau, Esq., Christopher Allery, Esq., attorneys for appellant; Lori Swanson, Attorney General, State of Minnesota, Julie Bruggerman, Mahnomen County Attorney, Minnesota, attorneys for respondents, Dec. 3, 2007.[2]

- State of Minnesota Court of Appeals, *Andy Joseph Roy, Appellant, v. Larissa Pauline Fineday, Respondent,* No. 06-1052, Appellant's Brief and Appendix, Frank Bibeau, Esq., attorney for appellant; Tammy L. Merkins, Assistant Becker County, Attorney, Minnesota, attorney for respondent, Sept. 24, 2007.[3]

- State of Minnesota Court of Appeals, *Andy Joseph Roy, Appellant, v. Larissa Pauline Fineday,* Respondent, No. 06-1052, Appellant's Reply Brief, Frank Bibeau, Esq., attorney for appellant; Tammy L. Merkins, Assistant Becker County, Attorney, Minnesota, attorney for respondent, Nov. 7, 2007.[4]

- State of Minnesota, County of Beltrami, District Court, 9th Judicial District, *State of Minnesota v. Joel Anthony Roy,,* Court File No. 04-K1-06-1026 Supplemental Memorandum of Law in

---

[1] *See also Greene v. Commissioner of the Minnesota Dept. of Human Resources,* 755 N.W. 2d 713 (Minn. 2008). The Minnesota Supreme Court held that requiring a tribal member to use tribal employment services rather than county services or accept a reduction in benefits had a rational basis and did not violate the Equal Protection Clause of the Constitution.
[2] *See also Morgan v. 2000 Volkswagen, License No.279, VIN No.3VWRA29M2YM125643,* 754 N.W.2d 587 (Minn. Ct. App. 2008). The court held that because the state vehicle-forfeiture law is a civil/regulatory law, the state lacks jurisdiction to enforce the statute against Indian owners of vehicles for conduct that occurs on the reservation.
[3] *See also* an unreported case, *Fineday v. Roy,* 2008 WL 3834980 (Minn. Ct. App. 2008). The court of appeals held that the lower court had jurisdiction to enforce state-ordered child-support payments from a tribal member.
[4] *Id.*

Support of Motion to Dismiss for Lack of Subject Matter, Anishinabe Legal Services, Frank Bibeau, Esq., May 31, 2007, to Randall R. Burg, Assistant Beltrami County Attorney, Beltrami.[5]

- *Antoine v. Winner School District* 59-2, No. 06-03007 (D. SD Ctrl. Div. Mar. 27, 2006)

- *Antoine v. Winner School District 59-2*, No. 3:06-cv-03007-CBK (D. SD Ctrl. Div. Dec. 10, 2007)

Documentary Film

- "Totah" produced, directed, and edited by Christian Regnaudot, 2002. "Totah" is the Indian name for the city of Farmington. The half-hour videotape describes the 1974 incidents where three Navajo bodies were found, the result of brutal beatings by three white teenagers, and explores whether or not similar racial tensions exist between the two groups today.

Public Comments

- Nov. 8, 2007 e-mailed comment of B. L. Sorensen, Navajo teacher, Farmington, NM. B. L. Sorensen reported that the local school district in the Farmington area has disparately few Native Americans in administrative positions such as principals and program directors. He alleged that two years ago a fully credentialed Native American principal applied for a job as principal at a middle school in Farmington, only to receive an interview for a bilingual teaching position.

- Nov. 8, 2007 e-mailed comment of Don Patrick of Gallup, NM. Mr. Patrick claimed the City of Gallup currently engages in discrimination by denying Native Americans employment in favor of whites and Mexican Americans. He further alleged that in the early 1970s there was a racist killing of a Native American activist by the Gallup, New Mexico, Police Department.

- Nov. 8, 2007 e-mailed comment of Dean Sam of the Walker River Paiute Tribe. Mr. Sam alleged that the Tribal Council running the reservation's court system (under 638 Contract Grant) has violated basic civil rights. The Council has twice banished a minor child from the reservation without upholding the child's rights. It has back dated court orders and falsified dates to win a case and used the court system to harm individuals that members of the Tribal Council dislike.

- Nov. 17, 2007 e-mailed statement of Warren Petoskey, member of the Little Traverse Bay Band of Odawa Indians and of the Lakota-oyate, and a tribal historian on the trauma Native Americans face generally and in treatment within the foster care system. Mr. Petoskey alleges discrimination by every town in which he has ever lived, by churches, public schools, and employers, including the State of Michigan's Department of Corrections. He asserts that he and his sons and daughters have been victims of discrimination. In working for tribes and state government, Mr. Petoskey claims he has never seen a reservation where its bordering towns did not openly display some prejudice regarding the Anishinaabeg on the reservation.

---

[5] *See State v. Roy,* 761 N.W.2d 883 (Minn. Ct. App. 2009). The court held that the state had jurisdiction to prosecute a tribal member on the reservation for felony firearms violations after conviction for terroristic threats (a felony crime of violence) and subsequent parole.

www.ingramcontent.com/pod-product-compliance
Lightning Source LLC
Chambersburg PA
CBHW081122280526

45787CB00007B/2940